Saving Free Trade

# Saving Free Trade
## *A Pragmatic Approach*

ROBERT Z. LAWRENCE

ROBERT E. LITAN

THE BROOKINGS INSTITUTION
*Washington, D.C.*

*Copyright © 1986 by*
THE BROOKINGS INSTITUTION
*1775 Massachusetts Avenue, N.W., Washington, D.C. 20036*

*Library of Congress Cataloging-in-Publication data:*

Lawrence, Robert Z., 1949–
 Saving free trade.
 Includes bibliographical references and index.
 1. United States—Commercial policy.  2. Trade
adjustment assistance—United States.  3. Free trade
and protection—Free trade.  I. Litan, Robert E.,
1950–    .  II. Title.
HF1455.L39  1986    382.7'1'0973    86-14705
ISBN 0-8157-5178-8
ISBN 0-8157-5177-X (pbk.)
9 8 7 6 5 4 3 2 1

iv

*For Alexandra and Ariel*

# Foreword

AS RECORD TRADE deficits in the 1980s fuel demands for increased protection from a tide of imports, American industry, the public, and Congress have advocated tariffs, quotas, and "voluntary" restraint agreements to forestall plant closings and save American jobs. This protectionist sentiment now threatens to overwhelm our nation's long-standing commitment to open markets, and with it much of the economic progress recorded worldwide in recent years.

In *Saving Free Trade: A Pragmatic Approach,* Robert Z. Lawrence and Robert E. Litan explore the complex and volatile subject of American trade policy. After considering arguments for providing aid to soften the impact of trade-related dislocations, the authors focus on the effectiveness of the two instruments used to provide this aid: the escape clause of the U.S. Trade Act of 1974, which allows domestic industries to receive temporary protection from import competition, and the trade adjustment assistance program, which was intended to direct aid to firms, workers, and communities injured by imports. They also examine the potential results of congressional proposals for trade reform and put forth their own pragmatic approach for saving free trade—an approach that can both relieve protectionist pressures and effectively and inexpensively promote the adjustment of workers, firms, and communities harmed by intense foreign competition.

Robert Z. Lawrence and Robert E. Litan are senior fellows in the Brookings Economic Studies program. They are grateful to Alice M. Rivlin, Robert Herzstein, Janet Nuzum, David Richardson, and Lawrence White, who reviewed the manuscript and provided valuable comments and suggestions. They also appreciate the dedicated research assistance provided by Tamara L. Giles. Finally, they thank Kathleen M. Bucholz, Jacquelyn G. Sanks, and Evelyn M. E. Taylor for handling the word processing, and Kim L. Orchen for research assistance. Jeanette Morrison and James R. Schneider edited the manuscript, and Carolyn A. Rutsch checked it for factual accuracy.

This study was supported by a grant from the Ford Foundation and by grants for the Brookings Center for Economic Change from the Alex C. Walker Foundation, the Xerox Foundation, and the General Electric Foundation. The Brookings Center for Economic Change is dedicated to finding ways of improving the productivity and competitiveness of the U.S. economy.

The views expressed in the study are those of the authors and should not be ascribed to any of the persons or organizations acknowledged above, or to the trustees, officers, or other staff members of the Brookings Institution.

BRUCE K. MAC LAURY
*President*

*June 1986*
*Washington, D.C.*

# Contents

## Figures

CHAPTER ONE

# Introduction and Overview

SINCE THE LATE 1970s, many Americans have seen the rising tide of foreign imports as a threat to the very existence of basic industries such as automobiles, steel, shoes, and textiles. Indeed, public opinion polls report increasing support for limiting imports of foreign products. Record deficits in the U.S. balance of trade during the 1980s are helping to translate that support into action by bringing Congress close to enacting blatantly protectionist legislation. Even the Reagan administration, strongly committed to free trade in its rhetoric, has at times succumbed to the heightened pressure. During its first term, the administration persuaded Japan to limit exports of automobiles to the United States and agreed to tighten quotas on imports of textiles. In its second term the administration has negotiated "voluntary restraint agreements" with a number of countries to limit their exports of steel to the United States.

Most economists have decried the apparent drift toward protectionism. They tirelessly point out that U.S. balance-of-trade problems have resulted primarily from a succession of record federal budget deficits that have drained private savings and have generated rising volumes of imports to meet domestic demands for consumption and investment. Eliminating such unfair trade practices as dumping or export subsidies that may be encouraged by other nations—while a worthy objective in itself—would scarcely make a dent in the U.S. trade deficit. The multilateral trading system is no more unfair to the United States today than it was in 1981, when this country enjoyed a positive trade balance in manufactured goods.

At the same time, however, there are reasons to be concerned about the long-range implications of the current trade imbalance. In the spring of 1985 the United States became a net debtor nation for the first time since 1914, largely as a result of the unprecedentedly high borrowing from foreign lenders that has helped to finance the trade deficit. Continued increases in debt owed to foreign nations will ultimately be paid for

1

by future sacrifices in American living standards through exports of goods that consumers here would otherwise enjoy.

Such a prospect sorely tempts lawmakers to turn to protectionist solutions to improve the trade balance. Some lawmakers embrace protectionist remedies because they have little faith that appropriate macroeconomic policies can either save the jobs of constituents in industries facing stiff import competition or promote the speedy reemployment of constituents who lose their jobs. Others believe that protection is a necessary or even desirable instrument of economic policy. For example, protectionists often claim that certain import-sensitive industries such as steel remain so essential to the economic vitality or the defense of the nation that they must be preserved at or close to their existing size. In addition, it is often claimed that jobs in industries facing stiff import competition must not be forfeited, because the workers who occupy them have few alternative employment opportunities.

In this book we reject the protectionist approach. During the past quarter century, the nations of the world have become highly dependent on each other for their economic success. In the United States the share of GNP represented by exports and imports combined increased from just over 10 percent in 1946 to 22 percent in 1984. In some countries, such as West Germany and South Korea, trade now accounts for more than 50 percent of economic activity.

Protectionism clearly threatens this interdependence, and with it much of the economic progress that has been recorded throughout the world in recent years. At a minimum, raising U.S. trade barriers would reduce the real incomes of American consumers, increasing the prices of both imported goods and the domestically manufactured products with which they compete. Protectionist measures would also reduce incentives for American firms to operate more efficiently, to hold down costs, and to develop new technologies and products. At worst, protectionism could lead to retaliation by U.S. trading partners, triggering the kind of downward economic spiral that the world suffered from in the 1930s. Of perhaps most immediate concern, curtailing imports from developing countries that are heavily in debt could severely strain an already fragile international banking system.

A central economic challenge, therefore, now facing all nations—but particularly the United States, which has been the linchpin of the liberalized trading order since World War II—is to find ways of enabling political systems to withstand or constructively divert pressures for protection. We believe this challenge is best met by pursuing a *pragmatic* approach to trade policy, one that provides safety valves or shock absorbers for protectionist pressures.

The pragmatic view recognizes that the transition to freer trade has its costs. For countries to move resources from industries in which they no longer enjoy a comparative advantage to more socially productive activities is often a painful process. But while the pain is almost always concentrated in particular industries and regions, the benefits of liberalized trade are generally dispersed among all consumers. As a result, democratic societies are peculiarly susceptible to temptations to reject or to slow the adoption of open trading policies. These temptations are strongest during recessions, when economic dislocations sensitize or acutely affect higher proportions of national populations.

Since the end of World War II the United States has used two mechanisms for relieving protectionist pressures. The first, the so-called escape clause, has allowed domestic industries to receive temporary protection from imports when they can prove to the U.S. International Trade Commission (ITC) that imports threaten or cause them serious economic injury. Modeled on Article XIX of the General Agreement on Tariffs and Trade, the provisions of the U.S. escape clause have been used since 1947 to protect more than thirty industries, ranging from the integrated steel industry to manufacturers of nuts and bolts. The American escape clause law, currently set forth in sections 201 through 203 of the Trade Act of 1974, however, has been the subject of continuing controversy and, as a result, has been frequently revised.

Since 1962 the United States has maintained a second type of safety valve, a trade adjustment assistance (TAA) program aimed at cushioning the impact on firms, workers, and communities adversely affected by significant import competition. This program, which is unique among all industrialized nations, has also repeatedly been modified. The stringent eligibility criteria written into the initial TAA legislation were so restrictive that no workers received any aid for the first seven years of the program. Accordingly, Congress expanded the assistance effort in 1974. In 1981, however, Congress reversed its course at the urging of the Reagan administration, which argued that TAA benefits duplicated unemployment compensation and delayed rather than encouraged adjustment. Although the program was briefly allowed to lapse in 1985, Congress once more extended it early in 1986.

Current concern about the trade imbalance has again prompted strong interest in making fundamental alterations in the U.S. trade laws. In this book we hope to contribute to informed debate by highlighting the principal problems in the escape clause mechanism and the TAA program and then by proposing what we believe are novel measures for correcting these flaws.[1]

Specifically, we suggest that the provisions of the U.S. escape clause would be more cost effective if declining tariffs were the sole form of relief that the president could impose to aid industries that succeed in proving they have been seriously damaged by import competition. All existing quotas and other quantitative restrictions should be converted to their tariff equivalents by auction; that is, all rights to import products within quota ceilings should be auctioned off to the highest bidders. Tariff rates should then be scheduled to decline over time. The revenue raised by these tariffs should be earmarked for assisting workers adversely affected by imports. In addition, a portion of the monies raised by converting existing quotas to tariffs could be used for compensating those exporting nations that would lose their "quota rents" (the benefits of being able to charge higher prices) to the United States and any other importing countries that participate in such conversions.

We recognize that the executive branch could nevertheless circumvent a tariff-only restriction by negotiating voluntary restraint agreements with other countries. Accordingly, we recommend that Congress take steps to discourage the use of VRAs. Congress can direct the Customs Service not to assist in enforcing other nations' export restrictions. It can also amend the antitrust laws to narrow or eliminate the defense of "sovereign compulsion" that currently shields from antitrust liability in the United States those foreign exporters directed by their governments to participate in export cartels.

Second, we suggest that the United States press for suspension of the compensation requirement in Article XIX of the General Agreement on Tariffs and Trade (GATT) in cases in which protection results from a recognized legal process and takes the form of nondiscriminatory, self-liquidating tariffs. Despite its good intentions, Article XIX has encouraged governments to avoid complying with the GATT escape clause and to turn instead to VRAs and negotiated trade agreements, such as the

---

1. Our views are shared in another recent study of the escape clause and trade adjustment assistance mechanisms. See Gary Clyde Hufbauer and Howard F. Rosen, *Trade Policy for Troubled Industries* (Washington, D.C.: Institute for International Economics, 1986). However, our specific policy recommendations, discussed in chapter 5, differ from those of Hufbauer and Rosen.

Multifiber Arrangement that restrains textile and apparel exports by numerous countries throughout the world. Suspending the compensation requirement in the narrow circumstances suggested here would go a long way toward making Article XIX a more cost-effective and useful provision of the GATT.

Third, we recommend that an affirmative injury finding by the International Trade Commission *automatically* trigger two different types of relief. Mergers of firms in beleaguered industries would be assessed under liberalized standards. These standards would recognize the full extent of the discipline exerted by foreign producers on U.S. firms, provided that the domestic industries are not shielded from import competition by quotas. Our antitrust proposal is somewhat different, however, than the administration's recent recommendation that the remedies provided by the escape clause be expanded to include an antitrust relief option.

The other type of automatic trade relief that we recommend is to extend trade adjustment assistance to displaced workers, but only in such a way that the benefits provided encourage rather than delay adjustment. Specifically, we propose that the primary component of TAA benefits consist of insurance against loss of wages. That is, workers displaced by import competition would be compensated for some proportion of any reduction in wages they may experience in obtaining *new* jobs, thereby encouraging those workers to find and accept new employment quickly. The proportion of the loss compensated could vary with the age of the worker and seniority in his or her previous job. A second component would provide extended unemployment compensation to workers residing in regions where the unemployment rate significantly exceeds the national average. The remaining elements in our proposed program would provide relocation allowances and assistance for retraining. Federal loans for retraining would carry repayment obligations tied to future earnings and collected automatically through the income tax system.

Even under highly conservative assumptions, this proposed program of trade adjustment assistance could be readily financed for at least a decade by converting existing quotas into declining tariffs. Such financing would be available even if a portion of the revenues from converting existing quotas were used to compensate exporting nations. As a result, there would be no financial pressures to impose new tariffs to fund the assistance program, although the president would still be authorized in the future to grant tariff remedies to domestic industries proving to the International Trade Commission that they merit relief.

Finally, we outline a new mechanism to ease the pain of economic dislocation for communities—a voluntary system of insurance by which municipalities, counties, and states can protect themselves against sudden losses in their tax bases that are not the result of reductions in tax rates. Under such a program, governmental entities choosing to participate would pay an insurance premium, much like the premiums firms currently pay for unemployment compensation, for a policy that would compensate for losses in the tax base caused by plant closures or significant layoffs. A targeted version of the program would provide such insurance only for trade-related plant closures or layoffs. Either version could reduce demands for protection by those local communities in which import-competing firms are major employers.

We begin in our next chapter by reviewing the principal arguments for targeting trade-related economic dislocations for special treatment. In doing so, we suggest that supporters of the various arguments can be classified into four groups.

—Protectionists tend to base their positions on two indefensible propositions. Their assertion that workers displaced for trade-related reasons should receive aid because they tend to suffer greater injury than workers laid off for other reasons has little empirical support. Their second assumption—that domestic industries should receive protection because they may somehow be essential—among other things fails to provide a principled basis for distinguishing those industries that should merit import relief and those that should not. Where production is essential for national defense, it should be supported directly through the defense budget rather than indirectly by protection.

—Supporters of managed intervention, a new approach to trade policy reflected in a number of congressional proposals to reform the escape clause, stress the need for government to participate actively in the rejuvenation of trade-battered industries by imposing requirements for industrywide reinvestment and modernization as a price for granting trade relief. This view is premised, in part, on alleged imperfections in the private capital market. These imperfections are supposed to prevent adequate capital from flowing to injured industries even after they receive protection from imports. This view is unfounded, and in chapter 4 we explain in detail why an approach to trade relief that imposes such conditions for reinvestment and modernization is ill advised.

—Advocates of pure free trade believe that the primary, or even exclusive, role for government is to provide the kind of general economic environment in which protectionist measures are least likely to be adopted. Government, however, is to take no special measures that single out domestic victims of international competition for special treatment. To be sure, some adherents of this view recognize that under certain conditions purely private decisions may lead to excessive reductions of industrial capacity, since private firms and laid-off employees do not always bear all the costs of industry shrinkage. In particular, the dislocation costs of other job-seeking workers in local areas increase when firms damaged by import competition add to the unemployment rolls with their layoffs. Nevertheless, advocates of pure free trade are skeptical that government intervention can effectively cure these market failures. While markets may dislocate prematurely, they argue, governments may prolong adjustment. In addition, firms and industries can shrink for a whole host of reasons unrelated to trade. Accordingly, advocates of pure free trade find it difficult to justify government intervention designed to slow the pace of industry contractions even where trade-related reasons are shown to be the dominant source of an industry's current decline.

—Finally, there are those who believe the advocacy of pure free trade mistakenly ignores the economic dislocations that free trade can cause. We agree with this group, and therefore favor the pragmatic approach of aiding potential losers from liberalized trade in order to help minimize both the demands for permanent protection and the willingness of lawmakers to supply it. Many believe that the availability of trade adjustment assistance has muted opposition by organized labor to liberalized trade policies. And Congress would almost certainly have halted the bilateral trade liberalization agreements negotiated in the 1930s and 1940s, and the GATT agreement itself, had not escape clause provisions been included. Moreover, the temporary nature of relief offered by the escape clause represents a less costly alternative to policymakers who might otherwise be tempted to resort to more permanent forms of protection—through legislation, voluntary restraint agreements, or orderly marketing agreements.

As with any government program, of course, targeted aid for dislocations resulting from international competition must be financed. Consumers must pay higher prices for both imported goods and competing domestic products when even temporary tariffs or quotas are imposed.

Additional taxes must be assessed to pay for trade adjustment assistance. Policymakers face the challenge of designing the two aid programs so that their benefits exceed their costs. At the close of chapter 2 we suggest that this challenge can be surmounted only if trade programs meet several conditions. Trade assistance must not be too easily obtained by domestic interests; it must be temporary; and it must be provided in a cost-effective form.

In chapter 3 we use these criteria to measure how the two instruments that have implemented the pragmatic approach to trade policy—TAA and the escape clause—have actually performed. Our conclusions are mixed.

On the one hand, the TAA program clearly has not effectively accomplished either of its two objectives, providing compensation and encouraging adjustment. The levels of assistance provided to displaced workers have borne very little relationship to the injury they may have suffered because of import competition. Meanwhile, the form in which assistance has been provided—in effect, extensions of unemployment compensation—has failed to provide incentives to displaced workers to find new jobs. Recently proposed amendments to the TAA program requiring workers to enroll in retraining programs as a condition for receiving TAA benefits would make little improvement. Because very few displaced workers who enter retraining programs subsequently find work for which they are retrained, the new requirements would continue to give these workers incentives to delay meaningful job searches and instead to sign up for retraining as a device for continuing to collect extended benefits.

On the other hand, the American escape clause law has performed well in several respects. The relief provided by the escape clause has proved to be temporary, as was intended. By statute, the president may grant protection for a period no longer than five years; thereafter, domestic interests must prove that renewed protection is merited. In fact, only three of the thirty-one industries that have won escape clause relief—motorcycles, specialty steel, and roofing materials—remain protected. Relief under the provisions of the escape clause has also not been easy to obtain. Although the legal standards that domestic parties must satisfy in order to obtain temporary protection have been weakened, only 58 percent of the domestic petitioners for relief since 1975 have been able to prove their case before the ITC. And only a quarter of the escape clause petitions filed since 1975 have actually resulted in some type of import relief. Finally, industries that have benefited from the protection of the escape clause have typically trimmed down to a level at which they could function profitably without further protection.

Nevertheless, certain troublesome features of the escape clause mechanism remain. First, even temporary protection entails a high cost to consumers for each job saved. Second, the current statute permits a president who desires to confer relief on an import-damaged industry to choose any one of three principal forms of protection—tariffs, quotas, or orderly marketing agreements. The latter two remedies are inferior to tariffs because, among other things, they have hidden costs and fail to provide an efficient means of encouraging adjustment.

Third, in the past quarter century the U.S. statute has departed from its original objectives and those of Article XIX of the GATT, which seek to ease the pain of adjustment caused by relaxing tariff barriers or adhering to other GATT obligations. Largely as a result of successive tariff reductions accomplished under GATT auspices, the current provisions of the Trade Act of 1974 no longer require domestic parties to establish that their injuries stem from adherence by the United States to GATT obligations. Instead the provisions allow import protection merely on proof of a causal connection between the importation of foreign products and the economic harm suffered by domestic interests. In its current form, therefore, the American escape clause is susceptible to abuse, a danger that would be intensified by proposals to relax the legal standard for proving that escape relief is needed.

Finally, the fact that presidents have denied relief to more than half the industries successfully proving import-induced injury to the ITC since 1975 has itself emerged as a problem. With ultimate relief so uncertain, lawmakers have been subject to increasing pressures by domestic interests to legislate costly quantitative import restrictions, which, unlike escape clause relief, tend to become permanent. Quotas and voluntary restraint agreements on imported beef, dairy products, and sugar, for example, have been in place for much of the post–World War II era. Although implemented through international treaties rather than through legislation, quotas on textile imports have been negotiated by successive administrations since 1957 because of the threat of congressional action. Indeed, the president's refusal to grant the American shoe industry relief after the ITC's September 1985 finding that it suffered serious injury from imports fueled congressional support for long-lasting quotas on imports of shoes, copper, and textiles. Similarly, congressional support for import protection for the domestic steel industry has driven four administrations to negotiate voluntary restraint agreements on steel imports.

In short, although in principle we favor the pragmatic approach to trade policy, we find much fault in the way it has actually been implemented. In chapter 4 we suggest that congressional proposals turning in other directions would produce even worse results, based on our analysis of how the escape clause process has operated and on the economic performances of domestic industries benefiting from some type of import protection during the past two decades.

Further movement in the direction of greater protection would not only damage consumers and threaten to create a retaliatory spiral, but would also fail even to accomplish its intended objectives. First, it would save few jobs. An analysis of sixteen industries receiving import relief under the escape clause reveals that only *one*—bicycles—subsequently returned to the levels of employment it had achieved before it was protected. And even in this case, many workers employed in the industry before protection was granted lost their jobs as domestic bicycle manufacturers moved their plants to locations with lower labor costs. Second, in many cases protection has not led to the restoration of domestic industries, which have continued to decline for fundamental reasons unrelated to import competition.

Equally dangerous are the proposals for managed intervention that would require recipients of relief under the provisions of the escape clause to adhere to specific commitments made as part of adjustment plans agreed upon by management, labor, and government. Setting conditions for aid presumes that the government—either alone or as part of a tripartite body with representatives of labor and management—can better decide what form adjustment should take and how to accomplish it than firms in the relevant industries and the capital markets on which they depend. In fact, given the political reluctance to abandon industries in trouble, it is likely that mandated adjustment would regularly take the form of substantial reinvestment in import-damaged domestic industries in the hope that new capital and modernized plants would restore competitiveness. This is precisely what occurred in 1984, when for the first time Congress imposed conditions for trade relief for the steel industry. Congress required the president to certify each year, as a condition for continuing any bilateral export restraint arrangements negotiated with other steel-exporting countries, that the eight major

American steel companies were reinvesting all their net cash flow in the steel business.

But the experience with the steel industry demonstrates why trade-related conditions should not be imposed. Since 1976 the steel companies that have recorded the best market performance—measured by returns to their shareholders—have been those that have reinvested the *least* in steel facilities. In fact, virtually every industry receiving protection under the escape clause has shrunk in size, including those industries that successfully modernized production facilities or developed new products. Had these industries been required to meet the same kind of reinvestment conditions that Congress placed on the steel industry in 1984, they would have been plagued with excess capacity and almost certainly would have been less able to compete successfully with foreign producers.

In cases in which industry conditions call for shrinkage of capacity, the tripartite negotiation process produces another danger—the likelihood of collusion. Because proposals for managed intervention would allow import relief to remain in effect only as long as the specified conditions are met, firms would have strong incentives to arrive at tacit, or even explicit, understandings about how they would share capacity reductions in order to ensure that all industry members continued to benefit from the protection of the escape clause. Although it may be in the public interest to facilitate mergers among firms in import-affected industries, consumers would not be well served by policies encouraging companies to coordinate their competitive activities.

In our concluding chapter, we outline what we consider a superior approach for improving the framework of trade policy. Our proposals, already foreshadowed above, do not reject the pragmatic view that has shaped trade policy among GATT members during most of the postwar era. Instead, the recommendations would correct the flaws in the programs through which trade policy has been implemented. We believe that these recommendations offer a far better way of effectively redirecting pressures for protectionist policies than either current law or the proposals for trade reform that are now being actively considered in Congress.

CHAPTER TWO

# Why Provide Aid
# for Trade-Related Dislocation?

ECONOMIC DISLOCATION is an inherent part of the competitive process. As new firms are created, others are destroyed; new technologies and products are constantly displacing those that are outmoded. In their continual efforts to reduce costs, some firms choose to relocate their plants, disrupting the lives of the workers and residents of the communities they leave behind. Other firms are so poorly managed that they may be forced to close or to scale back their operations significantly. Perhaps most important, fluctuations in the aggregate level of economic activity throughout the economy constantly buffet firms and workers.

Since the Great Depression, the United States has had a safety net to provide at least some protection to those adversely affected by economic events. Federal and state unemployment insurance programs now pay unemployed workers an average of one-third to two-thirds of their previous wages for at least six months following layoff.[1] Federal authorities have also become more willing to use stimulative fiscal and monetary policies to rescue the economy from downturns in aggregate employment and production.

The two components of this modern economic safety net share a fundamental feature. Like private medical insurance policies, which compensate individuals regardless of the reasons for which medical expenses are incurred, unemployment compensation programs and countercyclical macroeconomic policies provide protection to workers and firms against the condition of economic distress regardless of the specific causes that may produce it. Steel workers who lose their jobs as a direct result of import competition, for example, receive the same unemployment benefits as employees of semiconductor firms laid off because of a slump in demand for computers. Similarly, when the Federal

1. Lynn E. Browne, "Structural Change and Dislocated Workers," *Federal Reserve Bank of Boston New England Economic Review* (January–February 1985), p. 25.

12

Reserve decides to expand the money supply in order to help prevent a recession, it typically does so not in response to the difficulties being experienced by a single industry or sector, but rather because it believes that general economic conditions warrant looser monetary conditions.

International competition, however, is an especially visible source of dislocation that the United States has attempted to mitigate in three ways: through trade adjustment assistance (TAA), escape clause relief, and protection legislated by Congress. Supplemental aid programs for firms and workers adversely affected by trade provide a more targeted form of social insurance. They single out import competition from the many possible factors that can contribute to economic distress and use it as a trigger for special assistance.

On what basis can such targeted relief be justified? Advocates of pure free trade generally oppose programs that target aid for dislocation resulting from trade. They believe that international market forces tend to achieve the best possible social outcome and that when markets fail, government policies will most likely make matters worse. If aid is to be provided, they advocate that the same benefits be made available to all dislocated workers. For example, the Reagan administration has opposed trade adjustment assistance but favors general training programs, such as those under the Job Training Partnership Act of 1982.

Advocates of protection, managed intervention, and pragmatic free trade, in contrast, all favor aid programs for trade-induced dislocations, but advance different approaches based on different rationales. Proponents of protectionist policies generally support the concept of aid programs by advancing arguments based both on appeals to equity—that victims of import competition deserve special treatment—and certain justifications related to efficiency—that facilitating the revival of import-damaged industries through protection will increase national income. Advocates of managed intervention premise their reform proposals primarily on grounds of efficiency. And supporters of pragmatic free trade—the broad approach to trade policy we believe has the strongest conceptual and empirical support—rest their case primarily on a rationale of political efficacy, that is, that aid targeted to victims of import competition can prevent the adoption of permanent or long-lasting protection inimical to the interests of consumers.[2] This chapter

2. Michael Aho has discussed these three rationales—equity, efficiency, and political efficacy—primarily in the context of trade adjustment assistance. We use them here to

analyzes each of the underlying justifications for establishing special
government programs to ease trade-induced dislocations and outlines
the conditions under which such programs are most likely to be cost
effective.

## Basic Rationales for Intervention

### Equity-Based Rationales

In principle, government aid should be concentrated on the needy,
regardless of the sources of their misfortune. In practice, however, it
may be possible to justify targeted aid for import-related injury as a
second-best means of identifying those particularly disadvantaged.[3] For
example, one may rationalize providing supplemental aid for workers
displaced because of severe import competition if such workers were
generally less mobile and thus less likely than other displaced workers
to locate alternative employment. Similarly, assistance for trade-injured
firms or owners could be justified as a means of making the distribution
of income more equal if shareholders of those firms were particularly
disadvantaged by import competition.

The empirical evidence for the equity-based argument for targeted
trade relief, however, is at best mixed. On the one hand, worker
populations in import-sensitive industries appear to have slightly higher
proportions of women, minorities, and older workers, or groups that
traditionally have had higher unemployment rates than other workers.[4]
Similarly, recently displaced workers in the steel and textile industries,
in which import competition has been especially intense, have had

---

analyze trade-related intervention generally. See C. Michael Aho, "U.S. Labor-Market
Adjustment and Import Restrictions," in Ernest H. Preeg, ed., *Hard Bargaining Ahead:
U.S. Trade Policy and Developing Countries* (New Brunswick, N.J.: Transaction Books,
1985), pp. 87–112.

3. For a formal treatment of the use of trade policy to redistribute income because
other redistribution policies are infeasible, see Peter A. Diamond, "Protection, Trade
Adjustment Assistance, and Income Distribution," in Jagdish N. Bhagwati, ed., *Import
Competition and Response* (University of Chicago Press, 1982), pp. 123–49.

4. C. Michael Aho and James A. Orr, "Trade-Sensitive Employment: Who Are the
Affected Workers?" *Monthly Labor Review*, vol. 104 (February 1981), pp. 29–35.

greater difficulties finding other jobs than displaced workers in general.[5] Taken alone, this evidence could justify targeted assistance for victims of import competition as a device for reducing inequalities.

On the other hand, beneficiaries of trade adjustment assistance have not, on average, experienced significantly higher earnings losses from their bouts of unemployment than the recipients of unemployment insurance as a class.[6] Moreover, many trade-displaced workers in fact have had incomes higher than average. In recent years, for example, the U.S. steel and auto industries have been among the most seriously affected by foreign competition.[7] Yet in 1980 the average compensation for steel workers stood at 51 percent above the manufacturing average; compensation for autoworkers exceeded the manufacturing average by 33 percent.[8] As a result, it is not surprising that in these two industries displaced workers who have located new employment in recent years have suffered, on average, relatively significant reductions in earnings.[9]

Indeed, assistance for trade-related injury can actually worsen the distribution of income if the aid is provided in the form of protection from imports rather than direct assistance. According to one recent estimate, in 1984 U.S. restrictions on imports of clothing, sugar, and

5. Of the 5.1 million workers nationwide displaced between 1979 and 1983, 60.8 percent had found new employment as of January 1984. The reemployment rates for displaced workers in primary metals and textiles were only 45.7 and 59.8 percent, respectively. Somewhat surprisingly, however, the reemployment rate for displaced autoworkers was 62.9 percent, or 2.8 percentage points above the economywide average. See Paul O. Flaim and Ellen Sehgal, "Displaced Workers of 1979–83: How Well Have They Fared?" *Monthly Labor Review*, vol. 108 (June 1985), p. 5.

6. C. Michael Aho and Thomas O. Bayard, "Costs and Benefits of Trade Adjustment Assistance," paper presented at the National Bureau of Economic Research Conference on the Structure and Evolution of Recent U.S. Trade Policy, December 3–4, 1982, pp. 12–13.

7. Flaim and Sehgal found that of the 5.1 million displaced workers in January 1984, 220,000 had worked in the primary metals industries (mainly steel) and 225,000 had been employed in the automobile industry. Although certainly not all the unemployment in these two industries resulted from trade, both industries have been subject to intense import competition in recent years. Flaim and Sehgal, "Displaced Workers of 1979–83," pp. 12–13.

8. Colin Lawrence and Robert Z. Lawrence, "Manufacturing Wage Dispersion: An End Game Interpretation," *Brookings Papers on Economic Activity, 1:1985*, p. 96.

9. The mean annual earnings loss for former employees of the primary metals industry who were employed in January 1984 was $8,372, or 40 percent of their previous salaries; for transportation equipment workers, the average annual earnings loss was $4,160, or 20 percent of prior earnings. See Flaim and Sehgal, "Displaced Workers of 1979–83," p. 11.

automobiles cost low-income consumers nearly twice as much of their incomes as they did upper-income consumers.[10]

In short, the appeal to equity provides a weak justification for giving special assistance to firms and workers adversely affected by trade. While some workers displaced by imports may have greater adjustment difficulties than unemployed workers in general, on average the earnings losses of the two groups are not statistically distinguishable. In addition, import-related aid may actually lead to greater inequalities in the distribution of income.

### Efficiency-Based Rationales

With rare exceptions, freer trade provides gains for each trading nation that outweigh any losses because it enables countries to specialize in the production of goods and services in which they enjoy a comparative advantage. Under the principle of comparative advantage, nations can maximize the economic welfare of their citizens by concentrating in the production of goods and services where limited resources are best employed. They can then export the excess not consumed domestically and import other goods.[11]

Some economists, however, have advocated interfering with free trade on grounds of efficiency—namely, that under certain conditions, intervention will actually improve economic performance. In particular, three types of arguments based on efficiency merit consideration: that intervention is needed to preserve essential production, that it serves to protect so-called infant industries, and that it is necessary to compensate

10. Higher prices paid by consumers in the lowest income group surveyed ($3,000 to $3,999 in 1972–73) accounted for 1.56 percent of their after-tax incomes; for upper-income consumers (those with 1972–73 incomes $25,000 and above) the cost of the trade restrictions was 0.88 percent. See Susan Hickok, "The Consumer Cost of U.S. Trade Restraints," *Federal Reserve Bank of New York Quarterly Review*, vol. 10 (Summer 1985), p. 10.

11. This is the case even though a nation may have an absolute cost advantage relative to other countries in producing *all* goods. Paul Samuelson has explained comparative advantage by taking the case of the best lawyer in town who also happens to be the best typist. Given his limited working time, the lawyer should realize that his comparative advantage is in practicing law, leaving the typing to be performed by his secretary, even though the secretary is a less efficient typist than he is. Paul A. Samuelson, *Economics: An Introductory Analysis*, 7th ed. (McGraw-Hill, 1967), p. 647.

for private costs of dislocation that may not fully reflect total social costs.[12]

*Essential industries.* The first set of arguments favoring trade intervention suggests that the international marketplace can damage the nation's industrial structure. Specifically, by harming certain key domestic industries, trade can allegedly impair national defense. U.S. policymakers accepted this reasoning in imposing quotas on crude oil imports between 1959 and 1973 to protect domestic oil production.[13] Recently, advocates of protection for the American steel industry have resurrected the national defense rationale to justify restrictions on steel imports.

This argument is flawed. After the current defense buildup has been completed, the American steel industry will retain far more capacity than is necessary for protecting national security.[14] Perhaps more important, trade protection is an inefficient means of preserving the production capacity of an industry deemed essential to national defense.

12. There are other arguments for protection that we do not discuss here. For example, a country that is a large buyer or seller of a product can exploit its monopsony or monopoly position by limiting imports or exports in order to extract better terms of trade from its partners. See, for example, Harry G. Johnson, "Optimal Trade Intervention in the Presence of Domestic Distortions," in Richard E. Caves, Peter B. Kenen, and Harry G. Johnson, eds., *Trade, Growth and the Balance of Payments* (Rand McNally, 1965), pp. 3–34.

More recently, some economists have argued that protection can also be justified if it allows a nation to gain a dominant market position in certain high-technology industries in which costs can fall rapidly as production is increased. See J. David Richardson, "International Trade Policies in a World of Industrial Change," in *Industrial Change and Public Policy* (Federal Reserve Bank of Kansas City, 1983), pp. 284–95.

These are narrow exceptions, however, to the general rule that free trade benefits both exporting and importing nations. Moreover, the benefits implied by both exceptions can be negated by retaliation by other countries, which can make all nations worse off.

13. Section 232 of the Trade Expansion Act of 1962 allows the president to impose trade protection when imports of an article are found by the Department of Commerce to threaten national security. President Eisenhower, however, imposed mandatory oil import quotas in 1959 under provisions adopted earlier as part of the Trade Agreements Extension Act of 1955, which required the director of defense mobilization to advise the president whenever he believed that a product was being imported in such quantities as to threaten national security. Oil import quotas were abandoned by the Nixon administration in 1973.

14. By 1987, national defense needs are projected to require only 7.6 percent of iron and steel forging production and 5.2 percent of iron and steel foundry production. See U.S. Department of Commerce, Bureau of Industrial Economics, *1983 U.S. Industrial Outlook* (Commerce Department, 1983), p. xlii. See also Earl A. Thompson, "An Economic Basis for the 'National Defense Argument' for Aiding Certain Industries," *Journal of Political Economy*, vol. 87 (February 1979), pp. 1–36.

A far less costly mechanism is to pay for the capacity and necessary stockpiles of defense materials directly out of the federal expenditure budget.

Others have justified special government treatment by asserting a need to protect and support certain basic industries (again, such as steel) considered essential to the performance of other industries.[15] The government, they argue, must subsidize or shelter these industries from import competition in order to prevent the American industries that rely on them from becoming vulnerable to price hikes or supply disruptions.

The first problem with the argument for protecting basic industries is that it applies only, if at all, to those products for which international competition is weak, such as crude oil in the 1970s, when the OPEC cartel had effective control over world oil prices. Strong competition in the international marketplace assures a steady supply of imported products at competitive prices. With such competition, American purchasers should not be concerned that domestic suppliers may be driven out of business or forced to shrink capacity. Indeed, American business will suffer if government misguidedly imposes import restrictions on relevant inputs. Restrictions only raise the price on such products and thereby reduce or destroy any competitive advantage American manufacturers of finished goods may enjoy in world markets.

Nevertheless, it is sometimes argued that domestic capacity should be subsidized to prevent foreigners from gouging during periods of shortage. But this argument, too, rests on questionable grounds. Participants in private markets can foresee such possibilities as well as the government and are able to protect themselves in various ways—by agreeing to long-term contracts, stockpiling inventories, and using futures markets, among other devices.[16]

The rationale of protecting basic industries contains another flaw: no clear basis exists for distinguishing "basic" from "nonbasic" industries. Many industries produce goods for other industries—lumber for wood products, copper for finished metal products, cotton for textiles. There

15. Ira C. Magaziner and Robert B. Reich, *Minding America's Business: The Decline and Rise of the American Economy* (New York: Harcourt Brace; Law & Business, 1982), p. 337.

16. Only where political or macroeconomic externalities may exist is there a compelling case for government intervention, and even in such cases, stockpiling is generally more cost effective than protecting uneconomic capacity. See Barry P. Bosworth and Robert Z. Lawrence, *Commodity Prices and the New Inflation* (Brookings, 1982), pp. 132–59.

is no principled basis for singling out one or two of these sectors of the economy for subsidies or protection from imports.[17]

*Infant and recuperating industries.* Another classic rationale for protection is that new domestic industries need to be shielded from import competition until they can become viable international competitors. Given the developed nature of the U.S. economy, the argument for protecting infant industries is rarely invoked. Proponents of protection do, however, frequently claim that a major objective of trade policy should be to allow import-damaged industries some breathing room in order to recuperate and modernize.

Although it is rarely stated as such, the rationale for special trade assistance to rejuvenate faltering industries implies a major failure in the capital market. If an industry can be profitable once it has attained sufficient capacity or experience (an infant industry) or when it has modernized and retooled itself (a recuperating industry), what prevents it from entering the capital market to obtain funds to tide itself over until it can compete? The answer must be that private participants in the capital market are, for some reason, systematically unable to recognize these opportunities. But this proposition is difficult to accept. The United States has the most well-developed capital market in the world, with nearly 15,000 commercial banks, more than 2,100 insurance companies and pension funds, and highly talented and well-capitalized investment banking houses, let alone the largest network of stock and bond exchanges in the world. With so many potential suppliers of capital and such a highly sophisticated system of financial intermediation to channel funds efficiently to capital users, the market should not systematically fail to recognize and finance industries that could become competitors in the international marketplace. And even if such systematic errors occur, we are not aware that government officials or lawmakers have superior forecasting ability or, by releasing such information, that they cannot convince private participants of its value.

Others justify government support of efforts to rejuvenate industry by arguing that the recovery of individual firms may generate positive external benefits for an entire industry. In the case of underdeveloped countries in which capital markets remain relatively primitive, this argument may be valid. But even in these cases, the best approach would

17. For a related discussion of these issues, see Paul R. Krugman, "Targeted Industrial Policies: Theory and Evidence," in *Industrial Change and Public Policy* (Federal Reserve Bank of Kansas City, 1983), pp. 123–55.

be to provide direct production subsidies rather than to use costly tariffs or quotas.

*Market failures and dislocation costs.* Politicians who seek to intervene to protect domestic industries often maintain that by doing so they will save jobs, implying that the sole alternative to current employment is permanent unemployment. This assumption is valid only from an extremely short-term perspective. Given sufficient time, most workers will find alternative employment, albeit often at lower wages. Some politicians also claim that protection can improve the trade balance. In a world of flexible exchange rates, however, restricting imports will not create employment. Import barriers may protect specific job slots, but since they will cause the dollar to appreciate, they will also induce job losses and cause erosion in international competitiveness elsewhere in the economy.[18]

More sophisticated arguments for trade intervention therefore focus on the costs of dislocation. Ordinarily, market forces determine decisions to lay off workers, to scrap equipment, and to close plants or companies. The market will allocate resources to their most efficient uses, however, only if the firms and workers immediately involved bear all the costs of plant shutdown or worker layoffs and if the relevant actors respond to prices that accurately reflect social as well as private costs. Nevertheless, under certain circumstances other parties may bear some of the costs of scrapping capacity in depressed sectors, and government policies, market rigidities, and monopolies may distort prices. These market failures are frequently cited as grounds for providing special assistance to victims of intense foreign competition. Accordingly, each bears further scrutiny.

—Externalities and Public Goods. The costs of major plant shutdowns or large worker layoffs are often not confined to the parties immediately affected. When a local firm adds to the unemployment rolls with significant layoffs, dislocation costs of other workers and job seekers in the region may dramatically increase.[19] Because private firms do not pay these costs when laying off workers and shedding capacity, purely private decisions may lead to the premature shrinkage or elimination of

18. For an elaboration of this argument, see chapter 4.

19. See, for example, Harvey E. Lapan, "International Trade, Factor Market Distortions, and the Optimal Dynamic Subsidy," *American Economic Review*, vol. 66 (June 1976), pp. 335–46; and James Cassing and Jack Ochs, "International Trade, Factor Market Distortions, and the Optimal Dynamic Subsidy: Comment," *American Economic Review*, vol. 68 (December 1978), pp. 950–55.

industries. Targeted government assistance may be able to prevent unnecessary shutdowns, or at least slow the rate of decline.

—Other Policies. Other government policies may also inhibit the optimal adjustment to slumps caused by strong import competition. In a dynamic context a proportional tax on capital income will distort the adjustment process because it reduces incentives for private-sector decisionmakers to redeploy capital that is no longer socially productive.[20]

Imperfections in the unemployment insurance program also distort layoff decisions. Because tax levels for unemployment compensation do not fully take into account differences in layoff experiences among firms, many firms lack incentives to lower their layoff rates.[21]

—Inappropriate Prices. Price signals facing individual actors will also be inappropriate if they are set by monopolies in product or factor markets or when markets fail to clear in the short run. If, for example, wages have been set too high in a unionized industry that competes with imports under the initial protection of a tariff, removing the tariff could impose enough damage on the industry to lower national income.[22] If markets fail to clear, that is, if wage rates do not fully adjust to eliminate any labor surplus, layoffs in an industry experiencing a decline in demand can be excessive because wages elsewhere are too high to induce other firms to hire displaced workers.[23] In the short run, free trade will result in a decline in national income from an incomplete use of resources.

That each of the foregoing market failures may exist, however, does not necessarily justify the adoption of policies intended specifically for easing or preventing trade-related injury. If markets fail to allocate or to adjust resources because of inherent failures such as imperfect capital markets and externalities, the appropriate response would be to correct these failures generally rather than to single out trade-induced dislocations for special treatment. And these corrective policies may themselves be subject to imperfections, introducing distortions in their attempts to achieve conflicting goals.

These problems can be compounded by attempts to isolate trade-

20. See Michael Mussa, "Government Policy and the Adjustment Process," in Bhagwati, ed., *Import Competition and Response*, pp. 73–122.

21. See Martin Feldstein, "The Social Security Explosion," *Public Interest*, vol. 81 (Fall 1985), pp. 101–02.

22. See Paul R. Krugman, "The U.S. Response to Foreign Industrial Targeting," *Brookings Papers on Economic Activity, 1:1984*, pp. 89–92.

23. Harry Flam, Torsten Persson, and Lars E. O. Svensson, "Optimal Subsidies to Declining Industries: Efficiency and Equity Considerations," *Journal of Public Economics*, vol. 22 (December 1983), pp. 327–45.

induced economic injury for special treatment. As we show later, programs that ensure against trade-induced injury have discouraged the movement of resources into more productive activities. Temporary protection from import competition can discourage firms from shrinking their capacity, particularly if that protection takes the form of quotas, which guarantee domestic producers a certain market share regardless of their ability to compete. Similarly, by making adjustment assistance available only as long as unemployment continues, previous TAA programs have failed to encourage workers to search actively for new employment. Furthermore, trade assistance can actually attract labor to trade-sensitive industries and thus increase the pool of workers eligible to receive supplemental aid in the future.[24]

Finally, programs for assisting the victims of foreign competition often suffer from contradictory objectives. Arguments supporting industrial modernization could produce policies designed to accelerate the pace of change; at the same time, however, arguments stressing the external costs of plant closures and worker layoffs could lead to policies designed to slow the rate of adjustment. In principle, an omniscient planner could simultaneously apply some instruments such as investment subsidies to encourage modernization, while using others such as employment subsidies to prevent the dislocation that modernization might cause. But the mix of policies would have to be extremely complex and the goals understood with great precision.

The 1974 Trade Act, which provides the most recent authorization for temporary escape clause relief, implicitly reflects these contradictions. The act instructs the president, who decides whether to grant import relief following an affirmative ITC determination of injury, to consider among other factors in making his decision the "probable effectiveness of import relief as a means to promote *adjustment* [and] the efforts being made or to be implemented by the industry concerned to adjust to import competition. . . ."[25] The term "adjustment," how-

24. One recent study of the Pennsylvania labor market found that labor supplies and temporary layoffs increased in those industries that received TAA subsidies. Katherine C. Utgoff and Claire Hughes, "Labor Market Effects of Trade Adjustment Assistance" (Alexandria, Va.: Public Research Institute, Center for Naval Analyses, August 1983); and Maureen Cropper and Louis Jacobson, "The Earnings and Compensation of Workers Receiving Trade Adjustment Assistance" (Alexandria, Va.: Public Research Institute, Center for Naval Analyses, February 1982).

25. Sec. 202(c)(3). Emphasis added. As we discuss in greater detail in chapter 3, since 1947 the United States has allowed domestic industries that can show serious

ever, masks two fundamentally different and contradictory concepts. For some, adjustment entails slowing the shrinkage of domestic industries damaged by import competition, a rationale just discussed. To others the term implies moving resources out of import-sensitive activities and into other activities in which the nation presumably enjoys a comparative advantage in the long run.

### Political Efficacy

The Constitution of the United States treats international trade differently from purely domestic transactions. While it expressly prohibits states from burdening domestic interstate commerce, it explicitly endows Congress with the right to regulate international commerce. Specifically, Congress must approve all changes in tariffs, a right that it jealously guards.[26]

The asymmetry in the distribution of costs and benefits of freer trade presents a major problem for policymakers in our political system. Because many now recognize the high costs of protectionist policies, primarily those pursued in the 1930s, the United States has developed a strong ideological commitment to free trade. Nevertheless, the benefits of liberalized trade—lower prices and better products—are generally diffused among all consumers. In contrast, the burdens of open domestic markets typically fall disproportionately on import-competing industries, their workers, and the regions of the country in which they are located. In a political system responsive to constituent interest groups, elected officials ignore at their peril the need to show concern for and render aid to these victims of freer trade.

The American system for handling demands for protection has evolved from this interplay between the ideological commitment to open trade and the political necessity for responding in some manner to constituent pressures. Indeed, many of the ostensibly confused and uncoordinated elements in American trade policy can be explained as responses to

---

harm from import competition to obtain temporary tariff or quota protection as a way of gaining some breathing room to restore their international competitiveness. Whether such harm has, in fact, occurred is determined by the International Trade Commission. Where that determination is affirmative, the president has discretion whether to provide relief, and in what form.

26. Article I, sec. 8, of the Constitution states that "Congress shall have power to lay and collect taxes, duties, imposts and excises . . . [and] to regulate commerce with foreign nations."

these conflicting tensions. Policymakers need safety valves to pursue a
long-term strategy of free trade. Responsibility must be widely diffused
so that they may avoid the blame and deflect the pressure exerted by
interest groups to whom they must respond. Thus, for example, federal
lawmakers may support legislation requiring quotas or making provisions
for locally produced content to aid an industry, secure in the knowledge
that the president will veto it. But they can deflect demands for protection
by channeling them through an independent body—the International
Trade Commission. The use of such imprecise phrases as "preventing
injury" and "facilitating adjustment" in trade legislation fulfills a political
purpose, particularly when adjustment may actually mean closing plants
or dislocating workers in a given congressional district.

Nonetheless, political pressures for protecting special interests can
overwhelm the consensus favoring free trade. The dangers are greatest
during periods of general economic distress, which can produce legislated quotas (as in the case of the textile bill passed recently) or voluntary
restraint agreements or more formal agreements negotiated by the
executive branch but motivated by congressional pressure (as in the case
of quotas on automobiles, steel, and textiles). Safety valves that relieve
protectionist pressure, diverting it from the purely political arena, can
therefore be extremely useful. They can facilitate trade liberalization
and better enable lawmakers to withstand demands for protectionist
policies.

*Aid to facilitate liberalization.* Some circumstantial evidence suggests that the TAA program for trade-displaced workers in the United
States has, in fact, successfully blunted labor opposition to liberalized
trade policies. Aho and Bayard have observed that it is "probably not a
coincidence that the 1962 and 1974 TAA programs were components of
legislation authorizing U.S. participation in the Kennedy and Tokyo
rounds" of tariff reduction negotiations, and that labor opposition to the
product of the Tokyo Round, the Trade Agreement Act of 1979, was
minimal.[27] Indeed, a survey taken shortly before the passage of the 1974
Trade Act revealed that while most respondents were reluctant to support
trade liberalization, they voiced support for freer trade if affected
workers received compensation.[28]

Escape clauses allowing temporary exemptions from trade liberali-

27. Aho and Bayard, "Costs and Benefits," pp. 41–42.
28. Paul A. Laudicina, *World Poverty and Development: A Survey of American
Opinion*, Overseas Development Council monograph 8 (Washington, D.C.: ODC, 1973),
pp. 51–57.

zation agreements have also had similar effects. As we discuss in the following chapter, agreements for liberalizing trade that were negotiated in the 1930s and 1940s would probably not have gone forward if they had failed to make allowances for industries seriously harmed by tariff reductions. In particular, the general escape clause in Article XIX of the GATT was inserted because of congressional pressure on the president's trade negotiators. It is likely that Congress would have prevented the president from obligating the United States as a signatory party to the GATT if Article XIX had not been included.[29] More recently, Congress came close to enacting legislation in the early 1970s that would have rolled back import levels across the board. As we discuss in the following chapter, revisions in the U.S. escape clause law in 1974 substituted for this sweeping protectionist legislation and served as an outlet for congressional frustrations.

Outside the context of trade, compensation provisions have assumed a critical role in passing legislation in the broader national interest. In 1978 Congress concluded that in order to attract majority support for phasing out price and entry regulation of the airline industry, it would have to provide some protection for airline employees who might lose their jobs. Five years earlier, Congress reached a similar conclusion when it protected railroad workers displaced by the mergers and consolidations that the Regional Rail Reorganization Act of 1973 had authorized.

The apparent advantages of compensating the losers from open trade policies should not be overstated, however. Workers who fear displacement from lowered trade barriers will likely draw only limited comfort from the knowledge that they may be eligible for adjustment assistance, which is not guaranteed and will not, in any event, provide full compensation for the economic and psychological losses from job layoffs. Similarly, the prospect of receiving only temporary protection from import competition through the escape clause process may not deter firms in import-injured industries from seeking permanent protection from Congress. These caveats suggest that targeted trade-related aid may have a very limited effect in reducing demands for permanent protection.

*Mechanisms to relieve protectionist pressure on Congress.* Reducing lawmakers' willingness to support protectionist legislation or to press the executive branch to negotiate permanent quantitative trade restraints

29. Kenneth W. Dam, *The GATT: Law and International Economic Organization* (University of Chicago Press, 1970), p. 107.

constitutes a second important and generally less well recognized way in which trade assistance programs can lead to more efficient economic performance.[30] Legislators can avoid action on requests for protectionist measures if they can report to their constituents that other administrative remedies, such as trade adjustment assistance or escape clause relief, are available and should be sought. If the interests concerned fail to obtain suitable remedies through these other devices, lawmakers can deflect further demands for action by citing the refusals by independent fact finders to recognize the merits in allegations that imports have caused serious injury. Similarly, when some relief is granted, elected representatives can assert that legislative remedies are unnecessary. In short, by making available less costly administrative alternatives to legislated protection, Congress can call "heads I win, tails you lose" when domestic interests demand congressional response to import competition.[31]

The adverse congressional reaction to President Reagan's 1985 denial of import relief for the American shoe industry after the ITC's determination that shoe imports had seriously injured domestic producers illustrates the political consequences of not allowing protectionist pressures to be relieved effectively. In response to the president's decision, a storm of protectionist sentiment culminated in congressional passage of sweeping legislation that authorized long-standing quota protection for the domestic shoe industry and permanent quotas for textiles.[32] Although a strong protectionist mood had gripped Congress before the president's decision on the shoe industry, many observers credit the president's action with strengthening support for the legislation.[33] In short, the perception that domestic industries proving import-induced

30. See the discussion in chapter 3.
31. Thus, Congressman Donald J. Pease (D-Ohio) has recently observed in noting that trade adjustment assistance can diminish pressure for protectionist legislation, "If [congressional] members do not have something responsible they can support, then they are more likely to support something irresponsible." Quoted in the *CQ Weekly Report*, vol. 44 (January 18, 1986), p. 124.
32. The bill also directed the president to negotiate reductions of copper imports from other copper-producing nations.
33. See, for example, floor statement of Senator John C. Danforth (R-Mo.) in introducing the Trade Enhancement Act (S. 1860), "The administration's denial of relief to the footwear industry under section 201 and its opposition to trade adjustment assistance fuel the fires of protectionism." *Congressional Record*, daily edition (November 20, 1985), p. S15959. See chapter 4 for a detailed discussion.

injury may not receive at least some temporary relief can make it much more difficult for Congress to resist constituent demands for legislated protection.

*Summary: Trade Policy Approaches and Justifications
for Trade Intervention*

Protectionists emphasize rationales that we find to be extremely weak. Neither considerations of equity, arguments that a given industry is essential or basic, nor the rationale of saving jobs is tenable. None points to trade intervention as an appropriate response. Those favoring managed intervention stress the need for protection to allow and encourage rejuvenation, an argument assuming either that the government possesses information superior to that of the market—a highly questionable assumption—or that industrywide externalities are present, a condition difficult to verify.

Both pure and pragmatic free traders agree on the weakness of basing the case for trade-related aid on grounds of equity or efficiency. They both question using adverse trade conditions to distinguish worker dislocation and are skeptical that government can improve on overall resource allocation by using selective policies to intervene in international trade. They disagree, however, over the issue of political efficacy. Pragmatic free traders would agree to permit exceptions when in the long run freer trade would result. They would provide some form of compensation in return for trade liberalization. And they might agree to temporary protection in certain restricted circumstances. Ardent free traders would insist on free trade at all times.

## Criteria for Cost-Effective Trade Assistance

As we have suggested, there are two contrasting ways in which the federal government can intervene to alter the pace of adjustment. One approach counsels that special assistance be provided because it may slow the premature shrinkage of industries. The other suggests that assistance facilitate the transfer of resources to sectors outside the trade-affected industries. Because in any given case it is impossible in advance to determine which outcome is socially most desirable, policymakers face the challenge of designing trade-related remedies to allow flexibility in meeting either objective.

Designing flexible remedies is not an easy task in a democratic society, where political incentives make it difficult for elected officials to give up on any industry. This political difficulty will most likely lead to the assistance of many industries whose current distress signals a permanent inability to compete without government subsidy or import protection.[34] If it is not structured correctly, trade-related assistance will only delay the movement of scarce resources out of noncompetitive industries into activities in which the United States has a comparative advantage.

Policymakers face a second challenge: to structure any supplemental trade assistance so that it is cost effective. The history of targeted aid in other contexts, in which it has been difficult to restrict assistance only to the intended beneficiaries, highlights the difficulty of this task. For example, the model cities program, originally designed in the 1960s to assist only six communities, was subsequently expanded to cover more than one hundred cities. The Economic Development Administration, established to target aid only to depressed regions of the country, eventually extended eligibility for EDA assistance to about 85 percent of all counties in the nation.[35]

Efforts to target assistance for trade-induced injury are susceptible to similar pressures to expand the class of beneficiaries beyond the point necessary to accomplish program objectives. Import liberalization may threaten the jobs of only a small fraction of an industry's labor force, but to overcome resistance to the relaxation of trade barriers, a much larger pool of employees may have to be compensated. Thus it has been estimated that in the absence of the voluntary restraints limiting the export of Japanese cars to the United States in 1981–83, approximately 26,200 more autoworkers would have lost their jobs (above the 225,000 auto employees that were displaced during this period).[36] In practice,

34. Government policies toward the domestic railroad industries in the United States and Canada provide a recent demonstration of this tendency outside the trade context. See R. Kent Weaver, *The Politics of Industrial Change: Railroad Policy in North America* (Brookings, 1985).

35. Amitai Etzioni, "The MITIzation of America?" *Public Interest*, vol. 72 (Summer 1983), pp. 44–51.

36. For the estimate of the job impact of the automobile import restraints, see Robert W. Crandall, "Import Quotas and the Automobile Industry: The Costs of Protectionism," *Brookings Review*, vol. 2 (Summer 1984), pp. 8–16. The estimate for total worker displacement in the auto industry, calculated for 1979–84, is found in Flaim and Sehgal, "Displaced Workers of 1979–83," p. 13.

however, it would be difficult if not inappropriate to single out for special compensation only those workers displaced for trade-related reasons. Yet by compensating all unemployed workers in industries adversely affected by liberalized trade, a nation runs the risk that the costs of targeted trade-related assistance will outweigh any benefits that such assistance may produce.

This danger is compounded by the tendency of many political leaders, particularly during times when the economy is weak, to assign excessive blame to import competition as the source of economic problems. In recent years, for example, growing complaints have been registered in the United States about the perceived domestic dislocations produced by intensified foreign competition. In fact, however, other factors have consistently been far more important in determining the fate of particular industries. During the 1970s, fluctuations in domestic demand played a much more significant role than changes in foreign trade in explaining the economic health of forty-two of the fifty-two American manufacturing industries.[37] More recently, it has been demonstrated that between 1980 and 1984, changes in employment in a sample of seventy-three American industries were not correlated with changes in the degree of import competition, indicating that during this period, factors unrelated to trade played a dominant role in determining the economic fortunes of domestic manufacturers.[38] Clearly, a trade assistance program that fails to discount exaggerated complaints about the adverse effects of import competition can fall prey to the pork barrel syndrome that ultimately soured the model cities and EDA programs.

We believe it is possible to meet the challenges and to avoid these dangers by requiring any special trade-related assistance program to conform to certain criteria.

First, assistance should be provided only for workers and firms in industries where *serious* economic dislocations result *primarily* from import competition. A more relaxed standard is unlikely to be cost

---

37. Robert Z. Lawrence, *Can America Compete?* (Brookings, 1984), pp. 54–57.

38. Norman S. Fieleke, "The Foreign Trade Deficit and American Industry," *Federal Reserve Bank of Boston New England Economic Review* (July–August 1985), pp. 43–52. Significantly, Fieleke found that the electronic components industry, which enjoyed the highest employment growth in 1980–84 (21 percent), suffered the severest downturn in its net trade position (measured by a 9 percent decline in net exports as a percent of total industry shipments). In contrast, the railroad equipment industry, which experienced the greatest loss of employment (nearly 49 percent), improved its net trade position (increasing its preexisting trade surplus by 5 percent of total shipments).

effective. Because all imports injure domestic industries to some degree, trade-related assistance should be limited to those cases in which injury from import competition is serious. Otherwise, all domestic industries engaged in competition with foreign producers will be entitled to assistance.

Second, trade-related assistance must be *temporary*. As we have discussed, one rationale for aiding victims of import competition lies in the ability of assistance to prevent or mitigate dislocation costs resulting from temporary economic fluctuations. Similarly, if trade-related assistance is to be provided to encourage adjustment, it must be temporary. The transfer of resources among different industries can, after all, be accomplished in a finite period of time. Permanent aid would clearly be inconsistent with both justifications. Indeed, permanent assistance can discourage workers and firms from adjusting or from taking the necessary steps to restore the industry to a competitive position. The textile industry, for example, has benefited from some type of quota since 1957, and in 1985 it might have obtained permanent protection had it not been for President Reagan's veto of textile quota legislation. In recent years, however, protection has not only prevented adjustment but has actually attracted resources to the production of textiles and apparel. By the end of 1982, a third of all clothing and textile establishments in the United States had entered the business within the previous six years.[39]

There are no hard and fast rules for determining the length of the "temporary" period for trade protection. As discussed in the following chapters, the U.S. escape clause statute has arbitrarily chosen five years as the maximum relief period, although a domestic industry may seek a renewal period. The test of whether relief actually is temporary therefore turns on how often, if at all, domestic industries have obtained renewed protection after the initial period has expired.

Third, trade-related aid must be provided in a cost-effective form. To most economists this criterion translates into a requirement that workers and firms receive aid in the form of subsidies rather than through import restrictions. Subsidies are more cost effective than either tariffs or quotas on imported products because they do not distort the relative

39. In France, which like the United States has been a party to the Multifiber Arrangement that has restrained textile trade among many countries, more than 20 percent of all new manufacturing enterprises are engaged in the textile and clothing industries. See *Economic Report of the President, February 1985*, pp. 117–18.

prices of goods and therefore have no effect on patterns of consumption.[40] Comparing the cost of "saving" a job through import restrictions and direct subsidies illustrates this difference. Crandall has estimated that the voluntary restraint agreements that limited Japanese automobile exports to the United States cost consumers approximately $4 billion in 1983, while saving the jobs of roughly 26,200 autoworkers. These estimates translate into a cost for each job saved of $160,000 a year—more than four times the compensation of autoworkers who otherwise would have been displaced, assuming, of course, that such workers could be identified.[41] Estimates of the annual cost to consumers of protection in other industries run even higher, up to $1 million for each job saved.[42]

Several harsh realities, however, temper the theoretical attractiveness of direct subsidies as the preferred means of supplemental trade-related support. As we observed above, it is impractical to expect that only those workers displaced for trade-related reasons can be identified and given trade assistance. When all unemployed workers in industries seriously harmed by import competition must receive direct payments, the advantages of subsidies over protection can be significantly reduced. Programs for subsidizing firms in trade-injured industries might also fail to be as efficient as economic theory suggests. In principle, national income will be maximized only if those firms with the best prospects for competing in the world market receive subsidies. At the very least, subsidies should be distributed in a neutral fashion so that all goods of identical value produced in an assisted industry receive an equal subsidy. In practice, however, political considerations can easily distort the allocations.

Another practical drawback to direct subsidies is that they are politically difficult to fund, particularly when the need for assistance is most pressing. Pressures for protection are typically most intense during

40. However, the taxes that are imposed to fund the subsidies can distort relative prices.

41. Crandall, "Import Quotas and the Automobile Industry," p. 16.

42. The high figure is for the cost of voluntary restraint agreements on specialty steel during the 1980s. See Gary Clyde Hufbauer and Howard F. Rosen, *Trade Policy for Troubled Industries* (Washington, D.C.: Institute for International Economics, 1986), pp. 20–21; and *Economic Report of the President, February 1985*, p. 117. In chapter 4, we suggest that the typical estimates of the cost for each job saved understate the true cost of protection.

recessions, when budget deficits are at their peak and when Congress is most reluctant to fund subsidy efforts. For instance, appropriations for the trade adjustment assistance program have fallen dramatically since 1980, despite serious erosion of the U.S. balance of trade. And although some direct aid for firms has always been an element of TAA, the total amounts allocated have paled in comparison to the monies made available to displaced workers.[43]

Finally, potential recipients of subsidies themselves may resist them, preferring less visible means of government support such as tariffs or quotas. Subsidies can brand the firms that benefit from them as inefficient and needy, an image managements are reluctant to accept.[44]

Whereas in other contexts policymakers have avoided providing direct subsidies through various off-budget devices, often through loan guarantees,[45] import restrictions have remained the preferred off-budget means of assistance for trade-related problems. Where protection is granted, our cost-effectiveness criterion suggests that it always take the form of a tariff rather than a quota. Unlike tariffs, whose costs are transparent to consumers and lawmakers, the costs of quotas are hidden and thus more easily perpetuated. Perhaps more important, quotas are more likely to discourage adjustment and strengthen those domestic producers with market power by freezing the share of the domestic market open to imports. By doing so, quotas remove competitive pressure on the domestic industry as consumer demand increases. Finally, and not insignificantly at this time of budgetary stringency, quotas, unlike tariffs, yield no revenues for the government.[46] As we discuss in our concluding chapter, this advantage of tariffs merits particular attention in designing funding mechanisms for any compensation programs for trade-induced injury.

The foregoing criteria structure much of our subsequent argument. In the next chapter, we examine how well the two trade-related assistance programs operating in the United States in the post–World War II era—

43. See chapter 3.

44. For similar reasons, farmers have long resisted proposals to replace the current inefficient system of price supports and acreage controls with direct income supports.

45. Barry P. Bosworth, Andrew S. Carron, and Elisabeth H. Rhyne, *The Economics of Government Credit* (Brookings, forthcoming).

46. Recent estimates indicate that had the quotas maintained by the United States been converted to tariffs in 1984, the Treasury would have earned $3 billion to $7 billion in additional revenue. Hickok, "Consumer Cost of U.S. Trade Restraints," p. 3. See our discussion in chapter 5 of the revenue gains from converting existing quotas.

the escape clause and TAA—have conformed to these three conditions. We offer our own recommendations for reforming these two efforts in chapter 5, suggestions that would better meet all three criteria for cost-effective trade-related aid than either current law or other trade reform proposals that Congress is now considering.

# CHAPTER THREE

# U.S. Trade Adjustment Efforts in the Postwar Era

A PRAGMATIC APPROACH to liberalized trade has guided U.S. trade policy since the end of World War II. The fundamental objective of policy has been to work toward freer trade, primarily on a multilateral basis through the framework of the General Agreement on Tariffs and Trade (GATT). At the same time, the United States has institutionalized two safety valves for protectionist pressure—the escape clause for import-damaged industries and trade adjustment assistance (TAA) for workers, firms, and communities adversely affected by trade.

This chapter reviews the performance of these two instruments in light of the criteria for cost-effective trade intervention that we outlined at the conclusion of the last chapter. We find that the American escape clause statute, although repeatedly modified, has worked reasonably well but that it currently suffers from several flaws that merit correction. We assess the frequently altered TAA program more pessimistically. The TAA effort has largely failed to accomplish either of its two original objectives—to encourage adjustment and to provide compensation for trade-induced injury—and thus stands in need of fundamental overhaul.

## The Mixed Experience under the Escape Clause

For more than fifty years, American law has reflected the idea that domestic industries adversely affected by open trade require some breathing room in which to adapt to a liberalized trade environment.[1] This concept first appeared in bilateral trade agreements, then through executive orders, and most recently in legislation. An escape clause

1. The historical discussion in this section draws on an unpublished memorandum prepared by William W. Gearhart, Jr., assistant general counsel of the International Trade Commission. We gratefully acknowledge Mr. Gearhart's assistance.

mechanism was also incorporated in the General Agreement on Tariffs and Trade, the international agreement that has governed trade in goods among more than eighty countries since 1947.

Frequent changes in the provisions of the American escape clause, currently set forth in sections 201 through 203 of the Trade Act of 1974, reflect a continuing unease about how best to relieve political pressure for protectionist policies. Indeed, in each successive period Congress has found reasons for dissatisfaction. Now that Congress is again considering modifications to the escape clause law, it is instructive to review this experience. Contrary to the perception many may hold, the current provisions of the escape clause are far more favorable toward domestic interests than they once were. At the same time, however, the more than thirty years of experience with the provisions exposes a fundamental flaw. By allowing the president complete discretion in deciding whether to grant relief to import-damaged industries, the escape clause mechanism is in danger of losing its ability to accomplish its fundamental mission: to channel complaints from domestic industries about import competition out of the political arena and into the quasi-administrative process.

### Origins of the Escape Clause

Both the U.S. and GATT escape clauses ironically have their origins in the Smoot-Hawley Tariff Act of 1930, which raised tariffs in the United States by an average of 60 percent and, according to most economists, helped to induce worldwide depression.[2] President Franklin D. Roosevelt came to this conclusion early in his first term, and in 1934 he secured authority from Congress to negotiate bilateral reductions in tariffs and other trade barriers. During the following six years, he successfully concluded reciprocal trade agreements with twenty-two countries, accounting for about 60 percent of U.S. trade.[3]

Many of these agreements, however, aroused the concern of domestic industries, which feared increased competition if the Smoot-Hawley tariff rates were relaxed. These fears were allayed when various escape

2. For a history of the congressional deliberations culminating in the passage of the Smoot-Hawley Tariff Act, see F. W. Taussig, *The Tariff History of the United States*, 8th ed. (New York: E. P. Putnam, 1931), pp. 490–500.

3. Testimony of Cordell Hull in *Extension of Reciprocal Trade Agreements Act*, Hearings before the House Committee on Ways and Means on H.J. Res. 407, 76 Cong. 3 sess. (Government Printing Office, 1940), vol. 1, p. 7.

clauses or safeguard provisions were included in the agreements. Some provisions, for example, scheduled tariff concessions to expire in the mid-1940s, while others enabled certain agreements to be modified or terminated in the event of wide movements in exchange rates.

The predecessor to the broader provisions in the modern escape clause in both the General Agreement on Tariffs and Trade and U.S. trade law was a paragraph in the December 1942 trade agreement between the United States and Mexico.[4] This paragraph was later adopted virtually intact as paragraph 1(a) of Article XIX of the GATT:

> If, as a result of *unforeseen developments* and of the *effect of obligations incurred by a contracting party under this Agreement*, including tariff concessions, any product is being imported into the territory of that contracting party in *such increased quantities* and under such conditions as to *cause or threaten serious injury* to domestic producers in that territory of like or directly competitive products, the contracting party shall be free, in respect of such product, and to the extent and *for such time as may be necessary to prevent or remedy such injury*, to suspend the obligation in whole or in part or to withdraw or modify the concession [emphasis added].

The emphasized portions of the paragraph highlight the key conditions a country must satisfy in order to withdraw temporarily a previously granted trade concession.[5] First, the country's imports of a product must increase, either absolutely or relative to domestic production.[6] Second, this increase must result from a country's GATT obligations (primarily its tariff reductions) and must cause or threaten serious injury to domestic producers. Paragraph 2 of Article XIX, however, requires the importing country first to "consult" with affected exporting nations, a provision intended to encourage the various parties to negotiate some kind of temporary agreement to restrain trade so that domestic industries can

4. *Reciprocal Trade Agreement between the United States and Mexico*, Executive Agreement Series 311 (GPO, 1943), p. 13.

5. The GATT, in fact, contains at least nine different escape or safeguard clauses. In addition to Article XIX, among the most important are Articles XII and XVIII, which allow member countries to impose quantitative import restrictions to protect their balance of payments; Articles XX and XXI, which allow governments to adopt measures necessary to protect health and welfare and national security; and Article XXV, which permits countries to obtain a temporary waiver from GATT obligations upon agreement by a two-thirds majority vote of GATT members. As used throughout this book, however, the term "escape clause" is meant to apply solely to the provisions of Article XIX.

6. Although Article XIX does not explicitly state what it means by an increase in imports, the GATT parties at the Havana conference in the winter of 1947–48 agreed that the term was meant to refer to both relative and absolute increases.

adjust. If the parties cannot reach an agreement, paragraph 3 of Article XIX entitles exporting nations to retaliate in kind against the country invoking Article XIX. In practice, paragraphs 2 and 3 have encouraged nations seeking protection under the GATT escape clause to offer compensation to affected exporting countries. The compensation practice implies that if, for example, the United States imposes tariffs on steel imports under Article XIX, steel-exporting nations can expect the United States either to implement offsetting reductions in other trade barriers (say, by lowering tariffs on sugar or beef) or to accept higher tariffs imposed by those nations on their imports of American products (such as computers or airplanes).[7]

### The Initial U.S. Escape Clause

The American escape clause requirements and procedures were first set forth in three executive orders issued between 1947 and 1951. The orders delegated the task of investigating the effect of imports on domestic industries to the Tariff Commission (renamed the International Trade Commission in 1975), but they reserved to the president the decision of whether to impose import protection in cases where import-induced injury was found. While the orders were in effect, the president withdrew a tariff concession in only one instance—after the commission found that imports of women's fur felt hats were injuring American producers.

Because it was dissatisfied with the administration of the escape clause under the executive orders, however, Congress enacted the first escape clause statute in 1951.[8] That the Tariff Commission had, in a number of instances, simply dismissed applications for relief under the provisions of the escape clause without even conducting an investigation constituted a major source of the dissatisfaction. As a result, the 1951 legislation required the commission to initiate investigations and to complete them within one year, upon application by any interested party, by request of the president, or by resolution of either the Senate Finance or the House Ways and Means committees. The 1951 law set forth standards for conducting investigations that were virtually identical to

7. For discussions of the compensation principle, see Jan Tumlir, "A Revised Safeguard Clause for GATT?" *Journal of World Trade Law*, vol. 7 (July–August 1973), pp. 404, 408–09; and Kenneth W. Dam, *The GATT: Law and International Economic Organization* (University of Chicago Press, 1970).

8. Section 7 of the Trade Agreements Extension Act of 1951, 65 Stat. 72.

Table 3-1. Key Changes in U.S. Escape Clause Legislation

| Year of statute | Definition of "increase" in imports | Causation standard | Measurement of injury | Relief provisions |
|---|---|---|---|---|
| 1951 | Both absolute increases and increases relative to domestic production included | Established test that an increase in imports must "cause" injury to U.S. industry | Commission required to investigate effect of imports on domestic industry | Withdrawal of previously granted tariff concessions allowed |
| 1955 | No significant change | Test clarified (increase in imports must "contribute substantially" toward causing injury) | Commission prohibited from considering operations not involved with the product at issue | No significant change |
| 1958 | No significant change | No significant change | No significant change | Congress empowered to override by two-thirds vote president's refusal to adopt commission recommendation. Tariff increase of up to 50 percent allowed |
| 1962 | Relative increases omitted; only absolute increases to be considered | Test tightened (increase in imports must result in "major part" from prior concessions and must be the "major factor" in causing injury) | Commission required to consider health of all operations of a firm | Two-thirds vote replaced with simple majority for congressional override of president's decision (legislative veto). OMAs[a] allowed as a relief alternative |
| 1974 | Relative increases restored, in addition to absolute increases | Test relaxed (imports must be a "substantial cause" of injury) | Regional injury findings authorized | Expedited consideration of TAA[b] added as a relief alternative |

a. Orderly marketing agreements.
b. Trade adjustment assistance.

those in the executive orders and in GATT Article XIX itself.[9] If the commission made an affirmative finding, the law required it to recommend to the president whether the relevant concession should be revoked or modified, or import quotas established, for a period necessary to prevent or remedy the injury. Within sixty days the president had to implement the recommended relief or to advise the Senate Finance and the House Ways and Means committees why he had not done so. The law gave the president virtually total discretion: he simply had to decide whether import relief was "in the public interest."

As table 3-1 shows, Congress has amended the 1951 statute several times. In most cases these amendments have been designed to make it easier for domestic firms to prove they are entitled to relief. This trend began in 1955 when Congress made it clear that a finding of affirmative injury could be reached even if an increase in imports was not the sole factor contributing to the economic deterioration of a domestic industry.[10] In addition, in cases in which firms in an industry made more than one product, the 1955 amendments prohibited the commission from considering the health of operations not involved in the production of articles competitive with imports. This, too, was meant to liberalize standards for relief.

In 1958 Congress again amended the law to be more accommodating to domestic interests. It shortened the period allowed for completing investigations from nine months to six months. If the commission affirmed injury from imports, the amendments permitted the president to award a tariff increase of up to 50 percent (and not just to withdraw lesser tariff concessions resulting from trade agreements).[11] In an attempt to increase the likelihood that relief would be granted, Congress permitted a two-thirds majority of both houses to overrule the president's refusal to adopt the Tariff Commission's recommended remedy within sixty days of his decision. This provision stopped short of the Senate's proposed legislative veto—that a simple majority be required to override

9. Specifically, domestic industries were to be eligible for relief if, as a result of a concession under a trade agreement, imports had increased (relatively or absolutely) in such quantities as to cause or threaten serious injury. This assessment was to be based on an analysis of the production, sales, employment, prices, and wages of the domestic industry concerned.

10. Specifically, the 1955 amendments allowed a finding of affirmative injury where increased imports "contribute[d] substantially" to serious injury.

11. On duty-free items, a new tariff could be imposed that was no higher than 50 percent of the value of the items.

Table 3-2. *Experience of U.S. Industries under Successive Escape Clause Provisions*

| Item | 1951–62 | 1963–74 | 1975–85 |
|---|---|---|---|
| 1. Cases brought before the Tariff Commission or ITC | 116 | 40 | 57 |
| 2. Affirmative injury decisions | 41 | 8 | 33 |
| 3. Success rate (line 2 ÷ line 1) | 0.35 | 0.20 | 0.58 |
| 4. Affirmative injury cases for which industry relief provided | 15 | 2 | 14 |
| 5. Relief granted rate (line 4 ÷ line 2) | 0.37 | 0.25 | 0.42 |

Sources: Paul Richard Golding, "The Effectiveness of Escape-Clause Relief in Promoting Adjustment to Import Competition" (Ph.D. dissertation, Fletcher School of Law and Diplomacy, 1984), p. 69a; Jagdish N. Bhagwati, "Market Disruption, Export Market Disruption, Compensation and GATT Reform," *World Development,* vol. 4 (December 1976), pp. 989–1020; "Import Plaints Flood ITC," *Wall Street Journal,* October 22, 1985; and ITC reports.

a presidential rejection of relief—and of suggestions by various House members in 1955 that the president lose the right to decide whether to adopt the Tariff Commission's relief recommendations.

Even as amended, the 1951 statute reasonably satisfied two of the three conditions for cost-effective trade assistance that we outlined in chapter 2. First, the legal standards governing the commission's investigations helped ensure that domestic firms were entitled to relief only when imports were an important reason for serious injury. Indeed, between 1951 and 1962 the commission reached an affirmative finding in only 41 of the 116 relief applications filed (see table 3-2). Moreover, the two-tier process of commission investigation and presidential discretion for awarding relief further narrowed the danger that import protection would be too readily granted. From 1951 to 1962 presidents imposed import protection in just 15 of the 41 cases in which the commission affirmed that injury had occurred.

Second, as it was administered, the initial escape clause statute was reasonably consistent with our criterion for cost effectiveness. All instances in which presidents awarded relief resulted in tariff increases rather than quotas. Nevertheless, the 1951 statute tacitly allowed relief to be granted in the form of quotas. In addition, the 1958 amendment imposing a 50 percent ceiling on tariff increases effectively would have allowed particular tariffs to be rolled back to the levels prevailing in 1934 if the president chose to do so.

The 1951 law had another shortcoming: it contained no specific time limit on protection under the provisions of the escape clause. There was thus no assurance that the protection would remain temporary, as Article XIX had intended. Subsequent legislation remedied this problem.

### The 1962 Amendments

Completely reversing the protectionist course of its first two amendments, Congress tightened the escape clause law as part of the Trade Expansion Act of 1962, a sweeping law that President John F. Kennedy successfully persuaded Congress to adopt to give his administration broader authority to negotiate tariff reductions, particularly with member nations of the European Economic Community.[12] The escape clause standards were made more restrictive primarily because the 1962 act established a new trade adjustment assistance program for firms and workers that the administration believed would have a less disruptive effect on trade policy than would tariff increases granted under the escape clause.[13]

Four types of amendments to the escape clause that were adopted in 1962, which are summarized in table 3-1, reflected this new direction in policy. First, only *absolute* increases in imports, not increases relative to domestic production, were treated as increases in imports. Second, the amendments significantly tightened the causation requirement: an increase in imports not only had to result in "major part" from previous concessions, but also had to be the "major factor" in causing or threatening serious injury. Third, the amendments deleted the "segmentation" rule adopted in 1955 so that henceforth the commission had to consider *all operations* of firms, not just those involving the goods subject to investigation, in assessing whether the economic conditions of domestic industries entitled them to relief. Fourth, the act set a four-year limit on the initial period of escape clause relief but provided for an unlimited number of four-year extensions.

Not all the changes adopted in 1962 were antiprotectionist, however. A legislative veto requiring a simple majority replaced the two-thirds vote required to overrule a presidential rejection of the Tariff Commis-

12. In particular, the EEC was not permitted by its member countries to negotiate as a single entity unless tariffs were cut across the board, or in a linear fashion (with each tariff cut by the same percentage). The 1962 legislation, therefore, allowed the president to abandon the item-by-item method of negotiation used previously in favor of a linear method of negotiation.

13. See James E. McCarthy, "Contrasting Experiences with Trade Adjustment Assistance," *Monthly Labor Review*, vol. 98 (June 1975), pp. 25–30.

sion's relief recommendations. In addition, the 1962 act broadened the range of permissible remedies to include the negotiation of orderly marketing agreements, or bilateral quotas.

The more restrictive standards adopted in 1962 had their intended effect. The commission made no affirmative injury findings in the twenty-five applications for relief filed between 1963 and mid-1969. But because the eligibility standards for trade adjustment assistance were virtually identical to those under the 1962 escape clause, the commission also made no awards of adjustment assistance during this period.[14] Over the longer 1963–74 period the commission affirmed injury in eight of the forty actions filed; in only two of these cases did the president award relief.

### The 1974 Amendments and Current Law

Not surprisingly, Congress grew to regret the restrictive amendments to the escape clause implemented in 1962, and in 1974 it largely reversed course. The timing was not accidental. Given the severe recession in 1974 that followed the OPEC embargo, protectionist sentiment was strong. Indeed, Congress had previously come close to passing the Burke-Hartke bill, which would generally have rolled 1972 imports back to 1965–69 levels.

Instead of limiting imports, Congress successfully turned its fire on the 1962 escape clause. Domestic interests, of course, believed that relaxing the legal standards adopted in 1962 would enable them to reap some of the gains they were denied when Burke-Hartke died. Free trade interests, however, legitimately believed that difficulties of obtaining relief under the 1962 standards had induced domestic industries to seek voluntary restraint agreements, by which the United States and other nations could circumvent the formal escape clause procedures in their countries (and under the GATT).[15] Indeed, from Japan alone the United States had obtained VRAs covering eighteen products by 1974.[16]

14. Jagdish N. Bhagwati, "Market Disruption, Export Market Disruption, Compensation and GATT Reform," *World Development*, vol. 4 (December 1976), p. 997.

15. The notion that VRAs are voluntary is, of course, fictional. Exporting countries agree to them because they fear more drastic limitations on entry of their goods into foreign markets in the absence of the VRA.

16. These products included bicycles, thermometers, wood screws, gloves, silk fabrics, umbrellas, and tiles. Many other countries, including Canada, Mexico, most EEC nations, and Australia, also had VRAs with Japan during these years that covered many of these same products. Bhagwati, "Market Disruption," pp. 1000–01, 1006.

Congress expressed these protectionist sentiments not only by undoing much of the 1962 legislation, but in certain respects by favoring domestic interests more than it had in the 1951 law. For example, Congress reverted to the definition of an "increase in imports" adopted in the 1951 act, including relative as well as absolute increases. More important, the 1974 law relaxed the causation test in three significant respects.

First, the 1974 act removed the requirement that increases in imports must result from trade concessions. Henceforth, a domestic industry could be eligible for relief merely by showing that imports had increased (absolutely or relatively), provided that it also met the other requirements of the statute. Second, the new causation standard required only that an increase in imports constitute "a substantial cause" of serious injury rather than "the major cause." The seemingly minor change in wording was significant because the earlier standard required imports to be a more important cause than *all other factors combined*. The 1974 amendments required that imports be only a "cause which is important and not less than any other cause." Third, the 1974 act allowed the commission to reach an affirmative finding if it determined that import competition had seriously injured a segment of domestic production in a "major" geographic area. This was the first time that Congress had defined "domestic industry" on anything other than a nationwide basis.[17]

The 1974 trade law also significantly modified the relief provisions of the escape clause statute. It established new time limits for protection: five years for the initial period, with one extension of three years. The previous law had permitted an unlimited number of four-year extensions.[18] More important, Congress for the first time set forth specific criteria on which the president had to base his decision to accept or reject a recommendation of import relief.[19] Perhaps most interesting,

17. The Trade Act of 1974, 88 Stat. 1978, stated that in order to make an affirmative finding of regional injury, the commission had to determine that production in the chosen geographic region constituted a substantial portion of the national production of the industry; that producers primarily served the area; and that imports were concentrated in the region.

18. The 1974 statute also required that an industry that had exhausted its relief could file another escape clause petition, but only after two years had elapsed from the last day on which relief was last provided.

19. These criteria included the effect of the proposed import protection on consumers and the international economic interests of the United States; the impact on American industries of meeting any compensation requirements under international agreements;

given the current interest in including a procedure imposing conditions for relief into the escape clause statute, the 1974 law also required the president to consider the efforts being made by the domestic industry to compete more effectively with imports. As the Senate report on the 1974 legislation stated, "The escape clause is not intended to protect industries which fail to help themselves become more competitive through reasonable research and investment efforts, steps to improve productivity and other measures that competitive industries must continually undertake."[20]

Finally, the 1974 amendments broadened the range of remedies the Tariff Commission could recommend to the president. In lieu of the import relief measures allowed under previous law—tariff increases, quotas, or orderly marketing agreements—the commission could now recommend providing adjustment assistance. Although the amendments did not permit the commission to recommend providing *both* import protection and adjustment assistance, the president could grant import relief and recommend that any applications for adjustment assistance made to the Departments of Labor and Commerce be given expeditious consideration. The president's relief decision continued to be subject to a legislative veto, a provision subsequently nullified when the Supreme Court ruled in 1983 that legislative vetoes were generically unconstitutional.[21] In 1984 the mechanism was replaced by one allowing Congress to override a presidential injury determination by joint resolution, which, unlike its unconstitutional predecessor, can be vetoed by the president.

Since 1974 the experience under the escape clause statute has conformed in at least one significant respect to the intentions of the lawmakers who supported the 1974 Trade Act. Of the fifty-seven petitions for relief filed between 1975 and 1985, the International Trade Commission has found import-induced injury in thirty-three cases, a "success rate" for domestic industries of nearly 60 percent (see table 3-2). This success rate contrasts with the 35 and 20 percent rates in 1951–62 and 1963–74, respectively. However, as before, the president has continued to deny the ITC's recommendations for relief in most instances: in only fourteen of the thirty-three cases in which the commission has affirmed injury since 1974 has the president awarded some type of import

and the economic and social costs that would be incurred by taxpayers, communities, and workers if import relief were not provided.

20. *Trade Act of 1974*, S. Rept. 93-1298, 93 Cong. 2 sess. (GPO, 1974), p. 122.

21. *Immigration and Naturalization Service* v. *Chadha*, 462 U.S. 919 (1983).

ADJUSTMENT EFFORTS IN THE POSTWAR ERA                    45

protection. In five other instances, he has recommended expeditious consideration of adjustment assistance.

### Assessment of Current American and GATT Escape Clauses

In chapter 2 we suggested that an appropriate trade assistance program should meet three criteria: it should be provided only where serious economic dislocations result primarily from import competition; it should be temporary; and it should be provided in a cost-effective form. The current U.S. statute measures up favorably against these criteria in several respects.

First, as the above discussion makes clear, the ITC has recommended assistance only when imports constitute a substantial cause of injury. The escape clause has not provided easy and automatic import protection: table 3-2 shows that only fourteen of the fifty-seven petitions filed under section 201 since 1975 have actually resulted in import relief.[22]

Second, protection has remained temporary. Although thirty-one industries have received protection by means of the escape clause since 1951, only three—motorcycles, specialty steel, and roofing materials— are still protected. Significantly, few industries receiving escape clause protection since 1975 have obtained it again (see table 3-3).

Third, the ITC has also shown that it is able to decide escape clause injury cases on the merits, relatively free from political pressures. In a recent econometric study Baldwin tested the factors influencing the ITC's affirmative injury findings between 1974 and 1983, discovering that economic variables can better explain these decisions than political variables.[23] The economic variables, comprising the industry's average change in its rate of profit during the previous five years, its average level of net profits to sales, and its average annual change in employment, were statistically significant in Baldwin's equations. Those variables designed to proxy political factors, however, did not display statistical significance.[24] Furthermore, ITC commissioners did not tend to favor

22. Perhaps even more significant, between 1975 and 1979, only 3.8 percent of all manufactured U.S. imports were granted relief under the escape clause law. J. M. Finger, H. Keith Hall, and Douglas R. Nelson, "The Political Economy of Administered Protection," *American Economic Review*, vol. 72 (June 1982), pp. 452–66.

23. Robert E. Baldwin, *The Political Economy of U.S. Import Policy* (MIT Press, 1985), pp. 103–14.

24. These political variables included the commissioners' political party affiliations, the size of the industry seeking relief, the petitioners (whether labor or management)

Table 3-3. *U.S. Industries Receiving Escape Clause Relief, 1976–86*

| Year of complaint | Product sector | Years of protection granted | Type of protection granted | Further requests of ITC | | |
|---|---|---|---|---|---|---|
| | | | | Year | Type of case | ITC decision |
| 1976 | Specialty steel | 1976–80 | Quota; OMA[a] with Japan | ... | ... | ... |
| | | 1983–86 | Quota | ... | ... | ... |
| 1976 | Ceramic tableware[b] | 1976–78 | Tariff | ... | ... | ... |
| 1977 | Nonrubber footwear | 1977–81 | OMA | 1982 | Unfair trade[c] | Terminated |
| | | | | 1983 | Unfair trade | Terminated |
| | | | | 1984 | Escape clause | Negative |
| | | | | 1985 | Escape clause | Affirmative |
| 1977 | Color television receivers and subassemblies | 1977–82 | OMA | 1980 | Unfair trade | Affirmative |
| | | | | 1984 | Unfair trade | Affirmative |
| 1977 | Citizens band radios | 1978–81 | Tariff | ... | ... | ... |
| 1977 | High-carbon ferrochromium | 1978–82 | Tariff | 1982 | Unfair trade | Terminated |
| 1977 | Nuts, bolts, and screws | 1979–82 | Tariff | ... | ... | ... |
| 1978 | Clothespins | 1979–84 | Quota | ... | ... | ... |
| 1979 | Porcelain-on-steel cookware | 1980–84 | Tariff | 1986 | Unfair trade | Pending |
| 1980 | Mushrooms | 1980–83 | Tariff | ... | ... | ... |
| 1983 | Motorcycles | 1983–88 | Tariff-rate quota | ... | ... | ... |
| 1985 | Cedar shakes and shingles | 1986–90 | Tariff[d] | ... | ... | ... |

Sources: William R. Cline, *Exports of Manufactures from Developing Countries: Performance and Prospects for Market Success* (Brookings, 1984); U.S. International Trade Commission, *Operation of the Trade Agreements Program, 1984* (ITC, 1985), and earlier issues.

a. Orderly marketing agreement.

b. Industry reported in Cline, *Exports of Manufactures*, but not by ITC.

c. Unfair trade practices as used in constructing this table include dumping and export subsidies.

d. Complaint filed in 1985; relief awarded in 1986. In 1984 the ITC reached an affirmative injury finding in the case of carbon and certain alloy products. Although the president denied formal relief, he negotiated VRAs with certain steel-exporting nations.

the industries in which they had spent a significant part of their professional careers. Baldwin concludes, "it appears that the aim of the founders of the ITC to free the decisions of the agency from the influence of current political pressures has been achieved by and large."[25]

Fourth, protection under the provisions of the escape clause has been associated with considerable adjustment, although most of that adjustment has occurred through industry downsizing. Examining the experience under the escape clause more closely, Lawrence and DeMasi examined the postprotection performance of sixteen industries that have received some form of temporary protection.[26] The authors found that twelve industries adjusted successfully, in the sense that they could operate profitably without further protection, while in four cases it was too early to tell. In only one of these sixteen cases—the bicycle industry—was adjustment associated with an expansion in employment and production. More typically, industries contracted to a point at which they were no longer damaged by trade. Hufbauer, Berliner, and Elliott reached a similar conclusion that "special protection as practiced in the United States cannot, for the most part, be faulted for freezing the status quo."[27] The experience under the escape clause thus does not provide

requesting the relief, and the national origin (for example, Japan or developing countries) of the imports purportedly injuring the industry.

25. Baldwin, *Political Economy of U.S. Import Policy*, p. 111. Questions have been raised about the quality and consistency of the decisions made by the ITC. See Walter Adams and Joel B. Dirlam, "The Trade Laws and Their Enforcement by the International Trade Commission," in Robert E. Baldwin, ed., *Recent Issues and Initiatives in U.S. Trade Policy* (Cambridge, Mass.: National Bureau of Economic Research, 1984), pp. 128–53. For suggestions about making the methodology for determining injury more precise, see Baldwin, *Political Economy of U.S. Import Policy*, pp. 187–93; Gene M. Grossman, "Imports as a Cause of Injury: The Case of the U.S. Steel Industry," National Bureau of Economic Research Working Paper 1494 (Cambridge, Mass.: NBER, November 1984); and Robert S. Pindyck and Julio J. Rotemberg, "Are Imports to Blame? Attribution of Injury under the 1974 Trade Act," National Bureau of Economic Research Working Paper 1640 (Cambridge, Mass.: NBER, June 1985).

26. Robert Z. Lawrence and Paula R. DeMasi, "Do Industries with a Self-Identified Loss of Comparative Advantage Ever Adjust?" in Gary C. Hufbauer and Howard F. Rosen, eds., *Domestic Adjustment and International Trade* (Washington, D.C.: Institute for International Economics, forthcoming). Some of these case studies may be found in U.S. International Trade Commission, *The Effectiveness of Escape Clause Relief in Promoting Adjustment to Import Competition: Investigation No. 332-115 under Section 332 of the Tariff Act of 1930*, USITC Publication 1229 (March 1982); see also Paul Richard Golding, "The Effectiveness of Escape-Clause Relief in Promoting Adjustment to Import Competition" (Ph.D. dissertation, Fletcher School of Law and Diplomacy, August 1984).

27. Gary Clyde Hufbauer, Diane T. Berliner, and Kimberly Ann Elliott, *Trade*

substantial support for advocates of managed intervention. The evidence does not support claims that U.S. protection has necessarily remained permanent and has failed to encourage adjustment.

But while the current escape clause mechanism measures up to some of our previously outlined criteria, it has proved very costly to consumers. Hufbauer, Berliner, and Elliott examined consumer costs of seven recent escape clause actions, finding that on average such actions cost consumers $340,000 for each job saved.[28] Actually, the costs may have been greater because these estimates assume that the domestic industries sheltered by protection are perfectly competitive. However, current law still allows the president to provide relief to import-damaged industries not only in the form of tariffs but through quotas or their equivalents. As we discussed in chapter 2, quotas are a particularly pernicious form of protection. Among other things, they can reinforce oligopolistic pricing patterns in imperfectly competitive industries and, relative to tariffs, can delay the transfer of resources out of protected industries.

In fact, there has been a disturbing trend in recent years toward the use of quotas. Since 1975 OMAs have restricted imports of specialty steel (stainless steel and steel tools), color televisions, and nonrubber footwear (see table 3-3). In addition, following the domestic steel industry's successful escape clause action before the ITC in September 1984, the Reagan administration negotiated four-year voluntary restraint agreements with a number of steel-exporting countries.

An entirely different problem with existing provisions of the escape clause stems from the uncertainty, if not unlikelihood, that relief will be awarded when a domestic industry succeeds in proving its case before the ITC. As table 3-2 shows, the president has granted domestic industries import relief in only fourteen of the thirty-three cases in which the ITC affirmed import injury between 1975 and 1985. Although the rate at which relief has been granted has risen since 1975 (42 percent of the cases, up from 25 percent in 1963–74), the American escape clause process has since its inception consistently denied relief to more than half the domestic industries successfully proving serious injury from import competition.

The uncertainty of relief after ITC findings of injury constitutes a

*Protection in the United States: Thirty-one Case Studies* (Washington, D.C.: Institute for International Economics, 1986), p. 20.

28. These costs ranged from $55,000 for each job saved in footwear to $1,000,000 for each job in the case of specialty steel. See ibid., pp. 14–15.

Table 3-4. *Protection Granted U.S. Industries outside the Context of the Escape Clause and Unfair Trade Practice Laws*

| Product sector | Trade barrier |
| --- | --- |
| Apparel | Quotas (initially voluntary restraint agreement) since 1957 |
| Autos | Voluntary restraint agreement since 1981 |
| Books | Foreign-produced not eligible for U.S. copyright since 1891 |
| Dairy | Quotas (statutory) since 1953 |
| Meat | Global quotas and voluntary restraint agreements since 1965 |
| Peanuts | Quotas (statutory) since 1953 |
| Petroleum | Quota on national security grounds, 1959–73 |
| Shipbuilding | Use of foreign-built vessels in coastal trade prohibited by Merchant Marine Act since 1920 |
| Steel (carbon) | Voluntary restraint agreement, 1969–74; trigger-price policy, 1978–82 |
| Sugar | Quotas and import fees (statutory) since 1934 |
| Textiles | Quotas (initially voluntary restraint agreement) since 1957 |

Sources: Cline, *Exports of Manufactures*, p. 56; and Gary Clyde Hufbauer and Howard F. Rosen, *Trade Policy for Troubled Industries* (Washington, D.C.: Institute for International Economics, 1986), table 2.1.

problem because it encourages domestic interests to exert increased pressure on Congress and the executive branch for protectionist remedies that are generally more costly than temporary escape clause relief. As table 3-4 shows, legislated or negotiated protection has almost always taken the form of quotas or voluntary restraints rather than tariffs. Quotas exclude foreign competition at the margin and thus increase any market power held by domestic firms. VRAs may inflict even more damage by allowing exporting countries to prevent the entry of competitors with lower costs into the export market. Indeed, as we discuss in chapter 5, VRAs are often enforced by collusion among the exporters themselves, a practice effectively immune from antitrust attack under U.S. law.

Table 3-4 also shows that protection granted outside the provisions of the escape clause tends to endure far longer than the four- or five-year customary period of escape clause relief. Import quotas have been applied to sugar, peanuts, and dairy products in the United States for more than thirty years. Domestic shipbuilders have been shielded from foreign competition in coastal traffic since 1920. And most costly of all in terms of higher prices paid by consumers have been the quantitative limits on textile and apparel imports, set initially through the VRA agreed to by Japan in 1957 and since 1962 through quotas negotiated bilaterally under the auspices of the Multifiber Arrangement.

Congressional pressure for protection can be decisive even when a major domestic industry loses a case before the ITC. After the auto industry failed in its attempt to demonstrate import-induced injury in 1980, congressional interest in quotas and legislation requiring domestic content was sufficiently strong to persuade even the Reagan administration, oriented as it is toward free trade, to negotiate a costly VRA with Japan to limit auto imports. In earlier periods, too, VRAs have limited imports of Japanese products after the ITC failed to find serious injury under the escape clause statute.[29]

Voluntary restraint agreements are also undermining the effectiveness of GATT Article XIX, which has been criticized for reasons other than those applied to the American escape clause law. In particular, Article XIX has been interpreted as requiring that any temporary protection be imposed in a nondiscriminatory manner and that *all* countries adversely affected be compensated.[30] Not surprisingly, GATT members have sought to avoid the stringent nondiscrimination and compensation requirements by negotiating VRAs or other bilateral or multilateral restraint arrangements rather than invoking Article XIX, a development that prompted one observer nearly a decade ago to note that the GATT escape clause was more honored in the breach than in the observance.[31]

The circumvention of Article XIX has, if anything, increased. Between 1980 and 1983 the share of manufactured imports subject to nontariff barriers in the United States rose from 6 to 13 percent; for nations of the European Economic Community the share increased from 11 to 15 percent.[32] These barriers have had a disproportionate impact on developing countries. As table 3-5 shows, the EEC and the United States both subject larger fractions of their imports from developing countries to nontariff barriers than they do imports from other industrialized nations.[33] GATT member nations have recognized these trends and

29. Voluntary restraint agreements have been negotiated with Japan following negative ITC determinations involving bicycle parts, malleable cast-iron joints, raincoats, porcelain tableware, and rosaries. See Bhagwati, "Market Disruption," pp. 1000–01.

30. Gary Clyde Hufbauer and Howard F. Rosen, *Trade Policy for Troubled Industries* (Washington, D.C.: Institute for International Economics, 1986), pp. 55–61.

31. Gerald M. Meier, "Externality Law and Market Safeguards: Applications in the GATT Multilateral Trade Negotiations," *Harvard International Law Journal*, vol. 18 (Summer 1977), p. 499.

32. Wolfgang Michalski, Henry Ergas, and Barrie Stevens, "Costs and Benefits of Protection," *OECD Observer*, vol. 134 (May 1985), p. 18.

33. For a product-by-product listing of nontariff barriers maintained by seven major

Table 3-5. *Share of Imports Subject to Nontariff Barriers, 1983*

| Importing area | Percentage of imports from industrial countries affected | Percentage of imports from all developing countries affected |
|---|---|---|
| European Economic Community | 10.2 | 21.8 |
| Japan | 9.3 | 10.5 |
| United States | 7.7 | 12.9 |
| All industrial countries | 10.5 | 19.8 |

Source: World Bank, *World Development Report 1985* (New York: Oxford University Press, 1985), p. 40.

expressed interest in revising Article XIX to deter countries from erecting such barriers, thus far to no avail.[34]

In chapter 5 we outline an approach for amending Article XIX that would go a long way toward eliminating the incentives countries now have to circumvent the basic requirements of the article. Moreover, we offer suggestions for improving the cost effectiveness of the U.S. escape clause statute in ways that preserve rather than undermine the pragmatic approach toward freer trade that has characterized American trade policy in the postwar era.

## The Disappointing Experience with Trade Adjustment Assistance

In theory, directly compensating the losers from freer trade is more efficient than imposing tariffs or quotas on imports. The United States recognized this in 1962 when it became the first developed nation to adopt a program designed specifically to assist workers and firms injured by import competition and to encourage their adjustment to other activities.[35] The program was expanded in 1974 to include aid to com-

---

industrial nations, including the United States, Japan, and the major European nations, see William R. Cline, *Exports of Manufactures from Developing Countries: Performance and Prospects for Market Access* (Brookings, 1984), pp. 56–59.

34. Reform of Article XIX was a major item on the agenda of the last GATT negotiation, the so-called Tokyo Round. However, talks on safeguards issues reached a stalemate and were regarded as a significant failure of that negotiation.

35. Australia experimented with a trade adjustment assistance program for workers between 1973 and 1976. European countries and Japan maintain comprehensive labor adjustment programs that do not distinguish between trade and other causes of economic dislocation.

munities damaged by trade. In 1981 the program was modified significantly to tighten eligibility standards for worker assistance; as a result, the program has dwindled.[36]

It is widely acknowledged that the TAA program has failed to accomplish either of its two objectives. The program has also proved to be an expensive means for providing the political and economic benefits that we believe are the primary rationale for giving special assistance to victims of import competition. Assistance for workers, in particular, has actually discouraged adjustment while providing imperfect compensation, at best, for losses caused by import competition. Programs for assisting specific firms, meanwhile, have generally targeted those with the poorest prospects for recovery. As a result, much targeted aid has been wasted. Although recently proposed changes could lead to modest improvements, unless significant changes are made, the TAA program will likely continue to remain far less effective than it could be in facilitating a broad national commitment to free trade.

## The Initial TAA Program

After considering the idea for nearly ten years, Congress first authorized trade adjustment assistance for workers and firms as part of the Trade Expansion Act of 1962.[37] The act allowed workers meeting the eligibility criteria to receive readjustment allowances in the form of

36. Much of the historical discussion in the following sections draws on Charles R. Frank, Jr., *Foreign Trade and Domestic Aid* (Brookings, 1977), pp. 39–58; and Michael Podgursky, "Labor Market Policy and Structural Adjustment," in *Policies for Industrial Growth in a Competitive World*, prepared for the Subcommittee on Economic Goals and Intergovernmental Policy of the Joint Economic Committee, 98 Cong. 2 sess. (GPO, 1984), pp. 71–96. See also James A. Dorn, "Trade Adjustment Assistance: A Case of Government Failure," *Cato Journal*, vol. 2 (Winter 1982), pp. 865–905; and Steve Charnovitz, "Worker Adjustment: The Missing Ingredient in Trade Policy," *California Management Review*, vol. 28 (Winter 1986), pp. 156–73.

37. A widely discussed early comprehensive plan for targeting federal aid to import-affected workers was proposed in 1954 by David McDonald, then president of the United Steelworkers of America, as part of a report to the president and Congress by the Randall Commission. Legislative proposals based on the McDonald report were subsequently introduced in Congress in 1954 and 1955, and debated through the early 1960s. See John Lindeman and Walter S. Salant, *Assistance for Adjustment to Tariff Reductions* (Brookings, 1960).

The concept of trade adjustment assistance was suggested even earlier in the professional economics literature. See, for example, Otto R. Reischer, "Adjustment to Imports and the National Interest," *Journal of Business*, vol. 26 (October 1953), pp. 254–62.

supplemental unemployment insurance payments. These workers could receive up to 65 percent of their previous weekly wages or 65 percent of the average weekly wage in the manufacturing sector, whichever was lower. The combined total of the regular and readjustment components of the payments, however, could not exceed 75 percent of a worker's previous weekly wage. Workers received readjustment allowances for up to fifty-two weeks (sixty-five weeks for those over sixty years old). Payments could continue for an additional twenty-six weeks if a worker enrolled in a retraining program certified by the secretary of labor. The act also established relocation allowances for those who received bona fide offers of employment at other locations.

The initial TAA provisions also allowed eligible firms with certified adjustment plans to qualify for technical and financial assistance. To help them prepare the plans, the act made available technical aid to pay consulting services for market research, engineering, and research and development, and to aid in establishing employee training programs. TAA provisions also offered financial assistance in the form of loan guarantees (up to 90 percent of principal), direct loans (with maturities up to twenty-five years), and tax relief (carrybacks on operating losses for five rather than three years).

Under the 1962 program, workers and firms could prove their eligibility for benefits only by completing a time-consuming application process and meeting highly restrictive standards. The application procedure required those seeking assistance first to persuade the Tariff Commission that relief was appropriate and then to satisfy the separate requirements of the Departments of Labor (for workers) or Commerce (for firms). The legal hurdles at the Tariff Commission were the most stringent because they were modeled on the restrictive escape clause standards set forth in the Trade Expansion Act of 1962. Specifically, petitioners were required to show that imports of the relevant product had risen, that this increase resulted in "major part" from trade concessions, and that the increase constituted the "major cause" of economic injury. Those groups of workers in a firm who were not significantly involved in producing the relevant import-competing product remained ineligible for TAA benefits even if they might have been laid off because of the generally poor condition of their firm.

The eligibility criteria proved highly restrictive. Between 1962 and late 1969 not a single worker received assistance, primarily because of the requirement that any increase in imports had to be due in "major part" to trade concessions.[38] The requirement was especially difficult to prove because at the time the 1962 act was passed, the previous major tariff concessions had been made in the late 1940s.

It was not a coincidence, therefore, that some workers finally began to receive assistance under the TAA program only after the Kennedy Round trade concessions took effect in 1968. Yet even then the numbers remained small. Between December 1969 and April 1975, only 35,000 displaced workers received assistance, only 3,500 were provided any type of placement services or retraining, and fewer than 125 qualified for relocation allowances.[39] Even when assistance was provided, it often came too late to encourage adjustment—an unsurprising result, given the cumbersome nature of the application process. Frequently, by the time decisions on the petitions had been made, many recipients had found new jobs.[40]

The experience with the component of the initial TAA program that assisted individual firms proved even more disappointing. No firm received assistance until 1970, and through 1975, only $41 million in aid was distributed, mostly for domestic shoe, piano, and textile manufacturers. The stringent eligibility criteria ensured that only the weakest— and therefore the least competitive—members of import-damaged industries were assisted. And the application process was so cumbersome that firms generally received aid long after injury was sustained.[41]

### The 1974 TAA Program

The flaws in the initial TAA program impelled Congress to make substantial changes as part of the Trade Act of 1974. The Nixon administration opposed the modifications, arguing that adjustment as-

38. Adjustment assistance was separately provided to almost 2,000 displaced auto-workers between January 1966 and June 1968 under the Automotive Products Trade Act of 1965, which authorized the creation of a free trade area between the United States and Canada in automotive parts. Aid under this legislation was made more readily available than under the TAA program because it was mandated for a single industry and contained more lenient eligibility standards. See Frank, *Foreign Trade and Domestic Aid*, pp. 55–57.

39. Ibid., p. 53.

40. *Trade Act of 1974*, S. Rept. 93-1298. The elapsed time between the date of displacement and the certification of eligibility for worker assistance averaged twenty-two months. See Frank, *Foreign Trade and Domestic Aid*, p. 53.

41. The elapsed time between the finding of injury by the Tariff Commission and authorization of benefits was seventeen months, with the longest case taking almost thirty-eight months. See Frank, *Foreign Trade and Domestic Aid*, p. 50.

sistance for firms had proved so ineffective that Congress should have eliminated it and significantly curtailed adjustment assistance for workers. However, Congress believed that it could cure the defects in the original TAA effort and expanded the program in the 1974 Trade Act.

The 1974 legislation relaxed the eligibility criteria for adjustment assistance just as it weakened the legal tests required for escape clause relief. Specifically, it dropped the required causal link between an increase in imports and previous trade concessions. It also weakened the "substantiality" requirement so that petitioners had to show only that an increase in imports had contributed "importantly" to layoffs of a given group of workers. Furthermore, the act transferred certification authority for worker assistance from the ITC to the Labor Department, which was considered more receptive to labor interests.[42]

The 1974 Trade Act also increased worker benefit levels from 65 to 70 percent of previous weekly wages. For workers collecting unemployment insurance, the maximum combined ceiling on regular and readjustment payments was raised to 100 percent of average weekly manufacturing wages. The payment periods remained as they were under the 1962 act (fifty-two weeks plus an additional twenty-six weeks for workers in approved retraining programs); however, workers sixty years of age or older were automatically entitled to an extra twenty-six weeks of benefits.

Finally, the 1974 legislation added to the TAA program an entirely new assistance effort for communities able to demonstrate to the Department of Commerce that an increase in imports had "contributed importantly" to layoffs of a significant number or proportion of workers in the area. The legislation made aid available to such communities to develop adjustment plans. If the Commerce Department approved these plans, communities were eligible for technical assistance, grants, or loans to improve local public works and to attract new firms.

The 1974 amendments clearly succeeded in expanding the scope of the TAA effort. As table 3-6 shows, total benefit payments to displaced workers between 1976 and 1980 were more than fifty times the cumulative benefits awarded in the initial thirteen years of the program's operation. Worker benefit payments were particularly large in 1980 (topping $1.6 billion), mostly because of President Carter's decision to expedite the certification of displaced autoworkers. Total assistance awarded to firms

42. The act, however, required eligible workers to continue receiving benefits directly from their state employment security agencies.

Table 3-6. *Levels of Trade Adjustment Assistance, Fiscal Years 1962–85*

Millions of dollars unless otherwise specified

| Recipient and kind of aid | 1962–75[a] | 1976–80[b] | 1981–85[c] |
|---|---|---|---|
| *Assistance to workers* | | | |
| Number of workers certified | 53,899 | 1,313,349 | 179,689 |
| Benefit payments | 45.3 | 2,455.2 | 1,718.8 |
|   Readjustment allowance | n.a. | 2,433.0 | 1,656.3 |
|   Training | n.a. | 19.0 | 51.4 |
|   Relocation | n.a. | 2.6 | 10.1 |
|   Other | n.a. | 0.6 | 1.0 |
| *Assistance to firms* | | | |
| Number of firms certified | 36[d] | 972 | 1,624 |
| Technical assistance | 1.2[e] | 53.4 | 79.9 |
| Financial assistance[f] | 39.6[e] | 272.0 | 112.2 |

Sources: Charles R. Frank, Jr., *Foreign Trade and Domestic Aid* (Brookings, 1977), pp. 50–51; Michael Podgursky, "Labor Market Policy and Structural Adjustment," in *Policies for Industrial Growth in a Competitive World: A Volume of Essays,* prepared for the Subcommittee on Economic Goals and Intergovernmental Policy of the Joint Economic Committee, 98 Cong. 2 sess. (GPO, 1984), pp. 88–89; and unpublished data from the Employment and Training Administration of the Department of Labor.

n.a. Not available.

a. October 1962 through March 1975.

b. Includes transition quarter.

c. Through April 30, 1985, for workers and August 31, 1985, for firms.

d. From fiscal 1969.

e. From fiscal 1970.

f. Includes loans, loan guarantees, and grants.

also jumped dramatically. Assistance was never given to communities, however.

The expansion of TAA did not free the program from criticism. Delays in processing continued to plague efforts to assist workers. The Labor Department became bogged down in each case by attempting to determine whether imports constituted an "important cause" in the decline in sales suffered by individual firms and in isolating the specific groups of affected workers. The delays significantly reduced the effectiveness of the assistance payments in encouraging adjustment. A study by the General Accounting Office found that by the time they had received their first benefit payments, 71 percent of the beneficiaries were already back at work. Moreover, only 25 percent of the recipients were permanently displaced from their previous firms, while nearly 60 percent subsequently returned to their former employers.[43] Finally, the critics

43. The GAO report also found that nearly three-fourths of displaced workers who

argued that the method of assistance—supplementing regular unemployment insurance payments—provided an insufficient incentive for workers to find new jobs. Many local officials who administered the TAA program, in particular, believed that the higher levels of unemployment payments discouraged workers from accepting other lower-paying jobs until after unemployment benefits and TAA readjustment allowances were exhausted.[44]

## Recent Modifications to the TAA Program

In early 1981 the TAA program's continued problems attracted the attention of the incoming Reagan administration, which had made cutting domestic programs its highest priority. Although it did not seek to modify fundamentally the component of TAA that assisted individual firms, the administration persuaded Congress, as part of the Omnibus Budget Reconciliation Act passed in 1981, to tighten the eligibility standards for worker assistance and to change the method by which benefits were paid. In particular, the 1974 eligibility standard—that an increase in imports contribute "importantly" to a firm's decline in sales—was strengthened to require that imports be a "substantial" cause of injury. The payment system was altered to allow eligible workers to receive readjustment allowances only after their unemployment benefits had been exhausted, and then only up to a maximum of fifty-two weeks. The TAA benefits could still be extended another twenty-six weeks if a worker enrolled in a qualified retraining program. In either event the maximum TAA payment was lowered; it could no longer exceed the previous weekly unemployment benefit payment.

All these changes had predictable consequences. The number of workers who received benefits in 1981–85 dropped dramatically from the 1976–80 level (see table 3-6). The total volume of worker aid also fell substantially (the $1.72 billion total for 1981–85 conceals the fact that worker assistance in 1981 alone totaled $1.44 billion). The trends in the

were surveyed had not used any of the special employment services or the job search and relocation allowances. See General Accounting Office, "Restricting Trade Act Benefits to Import-Affected Workers Who Cannot Find a Job Can Save Millions" (GAO, 1980); and J. David Richardson, "Trade Adjustment Assistance under the United States Trade Act of 1974: An Analytical Examination and Worker Survey," in Jagdish N. Bhagwati, ed., *Import Competition and Response* (University of Chicago Press, 1982), pp. 321–68.

44. Dorn, "Trade Adjustment Assistance," pp. 887–88.

Table 3-7. *Employment and Retraining of Workers under the Trade Adjustment Assistance Program, Fiscal Years 1976–84*

| Item | 1976–81 | 1982–84 |
|---|---|---|
| 1. Number of workers receiving TRA[a] benefits | 1,320,685 | 76,316 |
| 2. Number of workers who entered retraining | 47,790 | 23,876 |
| 3. Worker retraining ratio (line 2 ÷ line 1) | 0.04 | 0.31 |
| 4. Number of workers who completed retraining | 17,255 | 11,055 |
| 5. Retraining completion ratio (line 4 ÷ line 2) | 0.36 | 0.46 |
| 6. Number of placements after retraining[b] | 3,560 | 968 |
| 7. Placement retraining ratio (line 6 ÷ line 2) | 0.07 | 0.04 |

Source: Unpublished data from the Employment and Training Administration, Office of Trade Adjustment Assistance, U.S. Department of Labor.

a. Trade readjustment allowance.

b. Placements as a result of retraining based upon specific job definitions used by state employment service agencies.

assistance program for firms were mixed, however. The total number that received assistance increased relative to the 1975–80 period, but total dollar levels of aid fell.

In our view, the reforms in the TAA program instituted during the Reagan administration have failed to make significant improvements. But the increased emphasis on retraining has had an effect. As table 3-7 shows, the fraction of all workers receiving trade readjustment allowances who entered retraining programs increased sharply, from 4 percent in fiscal 1976–81 to 31 percent in fiscal 1982–84. In addition, the proportion of workers who have finished retraining has risen. Nevertheless, the percentage of displaced workers obtaining jobs for which their retraining qualified them has fallen from the initially low level of 7 percent to the even lower level of 4 percent.

These figures suggest that the TAA program under Reagan has failed to cure the disincentives plaguing the previous TAA effort. In both 1976–81 and 1982–84, many displaced workers appear to have signed up for retraining merely as a way of continuing to collect trade readjustment benefits. Moreover, the figures in table 3-7 indicate that despite the retraining incentives that have existed for more than a decade, most trade-displaced workers still have not sought retraining. For many of these workers, the new method of paying readjustment allowances only after regular unemployment benefits have been exhausted has only discouraged efforts to locate new employment opportunities quickly.

A second problem with both the Reagan-era and earlier TAA programs is that they have not compensated fully for the economic losses that trade-displaced workers have actually sustained. In principle, those losses equal the total earnings missed because of unemployment plus the decline in earnings in subsequent employment. For example, a steelworker who is laid off because of import competition and must eventually accept a job as a cook not only loses income during unemployment but also loses the value of his or her unutilized steelmaking skills, including forfeited "human capital" and accumulated seniority.

Current and previous formulas for trade readjustment allowances have considered only the first of these components of earnings loss. That is, TRA payments have historically been tied to the unemployment insurance system and have not reflected declines in earnings capacities of workers in subsequent employment. Two individuals who are unemployed for the same length of time may ultimately find new jobs paying greatly different wages, but under the prevailing formulas both receive the same amount of assistance.

A third problem has stemmed from excessively strict certification requirements for workers. The legislation authorizing TAA benefits has allowed only those groups of a given firm's workers that sustain significant numbers of layoffs from import competition to be certified as eligible for aid. Consequently, the Labor Department has been required to undertake time-consuming investigations not only into the effects of imports on individual firms but into the effects *within* firms. The department must then isolate which specific groups of workers may be entitled to assistance. We argue in chapter 5 that if readjustment allowances are provided in a fashion that encourages rather than delays worker adjustment, the eligibility criteria for TAA benefits do not need to be so narrow.

Finally, the shrinkage in the size of the TAA program during the Reagan years has severely diminished the effectiveness of direct assistance as a shock absorber for political pressure demanding protectionist measures. Indeed, the reductions in total benefits could not have occurred at a worse time. As figure 3-1 shows, total readjustment assistance payments have fallen dramatically since 1981. During the same period the U.S. current account balance deteriorated sharply, from a small surplus in 1981 to a deficit exceeding $100 billion in 1984, a development that has intensified demands for legislation to restrict the access of foreign firms to the American market.

*Recent Proposals to Change TAA*

In 1985 Congress considered but did not adopt a new trade adjustment assistance program proposed by Senators William V. Roth, Jr. (R-Del.) and Daniel P. Moynihan (D-N.Y.) and Congressman Donald J. Pease

Figure 3-1. *Trade Readjustment Allowances and Current Account Balance, 1975–84*[a]

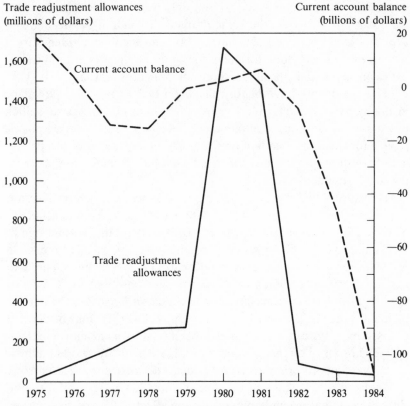

Trade readjustment allowances
(millions of dollars)

Current account balance
(billions of dollars)

Source: Robert Z. Lawrence and Robert E. Litan, "Living with the Trade Deficit: Adjustment Strategies to Preserve Free Trade," *Brookings Review*, vol. 4 (Fall 1985), p. 9.

a. Trade readjustment allowances based on fiscal years, trade balances on calendar years.

(D-Ohio). The new approach would have reemphasized the importance of retraining by requiring workers to enroll in or have completed a training program as a condition for receiving benefits up to a maximum of seventy-eight weeks. Workers could finance their retraining with a $4,000 voucher redeemable in a variety of programs, including those under the Job Training Partnership Act, those approved by the secretary of labor, and those conducted without federal support by private firms. To insulate the program against budget pressures, the new plan would allow the president to set an across-the-board import fee of up to 1 percent to finance the benefits.[45]

45. Because the import fee more than likely violates current GATT rules, the new

The TAA program continues to provide general technical assistance and some direct loans and loan guarantees. Providing loans, however, is of questionable value. Direct financial assistance for individual firms has long been suspect because it has been provided as a last resort to companies so troubled that they have been unable to obtain financing elsewhere. These firms generally prove to be the least able of all industry members to survive, as demonstrated by the high default rates on loans granted to recipients of direct assistance.[46] In contrast, technical assistance provided under TAA has been more far-reaching, touching seventy to eighty times as many firms as have received direct financial assistance. Significantly, 85 percent of all firms that received technical aid under TAA remained in business as of 1983.[47]

In early 1986 Congress extended TAA without the revisions proposed in the Roth-Moynihan-Pease bill. Nevertheless, Congress is again considering reforms in the TAA program in 1986. If enacted, the new program recommended by Senators Roth and Moynihan and Congressman Pease would help fill the void in the existing worker retraining effort. But we fear that the component of the proposed program requiring retraining would give both retraining and trade adjustment assistance bad names. Retraining is most effective when it is undertaken voluntarily by workers who want new skills and who are willing to pay at least some of the cost of acquiring them.[48] If, however, training is mandatory—that is, if it is a condition for receiving supplemental readjustment allowances—then many workers will enroll simply as a way of obtaining added benefits. Indeed, as table 3-7 shows, experience indicates that an

program directs the president to obtain GATT approval for the concept of using small general import fees to fund adjustment assistance. If the president fails to obtain GATT approval, the fee automatically goes into effect in October 1989 (otherwise becoming effective as soon as GATT approval is accomplished).

46. Approximately half of all loan recipients under the TAA program between 1976 and 1981 were in default by the end of 1981. By March 1983, 58 percent of all outstanding TAA loans were in default or liquidation, or required special servicing. Significantly, between 1972 and 1983, only five loans, totaling $3.1 million, had been fully paid back. See testimony of Lyle Ryter in *Oversight of Trade Adjustment Assistance Programs and Authorization of Appropriations for U.S. Trade Representative, International Trade Commission, and Customs Service*, Hearings before the Subcommittee on International Trade of the Senate Committee on Finance, 98 Cong. 1 sess. (GPO, 1983), p. 231.

47. See testimony of Harold W. Williams in *Oversight of Trade Adjustment*, Hearings, p. 305.

48. For an excellent recent review of training programs and their effectiveness, see Anthony Patrick Carnevale, *Jobs for the Nation: Challenges for a Society Based on Work* (Alexandria, Va.: American Society for Training and Development, 1985), pp. 231–51.

overwhelming proportion of workers who enter retraining programs will probably do so in order to receive supplemental benefits and thereby delay their search for new employment. The generous $4,000 vouchers, which would enable many workers to obtain retraining at extremely low cost and perhaps for free, could exacerbate this problem.

We outline in our concluding chapter a more cost-effective way of redesigning the TAA program. The unemployment insurance model of payment for trade-related supplemental benefits should be abandoned in favor of a payment system that encourages workers to find new jobs. Training programs should remain voluntary. And while the government should provide workers with the necessary financing, it should in turn oblige them to share some portion of their gains from retraining.

# CHAPTER FOUR

# Congressional Plans to Reform the Adjustment Process

CONGRESSIONAL INTEREST in reforming the trade laws has intensified, and given the high and rising deficit in the U.S. balance of trade, sentiment runs strongly toward protectionist measures. At the close of its 1985 session, the Ninety-ninth Congress passed legislation that, had it been signed by the president, would have set permanent or long-lasting quotas on imports of textiles and shoes and would have directed the president to negotiate restraints on foreign copper exports. The textile and apparel quotas, in particular, would have limited imports to a considerably greater degree than the existing constraints of the Multifiber Arrangement. Although President Reagan vetoed the legislation, proponents could succeed in attracting enough votes to override the veto in 1986, particularly if American textile interests do not perceive the new rules that emerge from negotiations to extend the Multifiber Arrangement to be sufficiently restrictive.[1]

The protectionist mood has also once again prompted strong congressional interest in changing the provisions of the U.S. escape clause. A number of so-called omnibus trade proposals that contain such amendments have attracted considerable attention: the Trade Enhancement Act of 1985, a bipartisan trade initiative introduced in the Senate by Senator John C. Danforth (R-Mo.) and more than thirty cosponsors (S. 1860); the Trade Expansion Act of 1986, introduced by Senator Lawton Chiles (D-Fla.) and seven cosponsors (S. 2033); the Trade Partnership Act of 1985, sponsored by the Republican leadership of the House (H.R. 3522); the Trade Law Modernization Act, reported out of the House Energy and Commerce Committee in November 1985 (H.R. 3777); and the Comprehensive Trade Policy Reform Act (H.R. 4750),

1. In an unusual move, Congress delayed the vote on the motion to override the president's veto until August 6, 1986, shortly after the United States is expected to complete talks on extending the Multifiber Arrangement.

Table 4-1. *Escape Clause Relief Programs under Current U.S. Law and Proposed Alternatives*

| Legislation | Mandatory remedies | Discretionary remedies |
|---|---|---|
| Current law | None | Gives president options of tariffs, quotas, OMAs, or expedited consideration of TAA petitions |
| Comprehensive Trade Policy Reform Act of 1986 (H.R. 4750) | None | Allows tariffs and quotas (which can be auctioned off if implemented) |
| Trade Enhancement Act of 1985 (S. 1860) | Mandates relief recommended by ITC if ITC accepts adjustment plan, subject to rapid congressional approval of alternative relief | Otherwise, retains presidential discretion as under current law |
| Trade Expansion Act of 1986 (S. 2033) | Mandates relief recommended by ITC, subject to presidential veto | Allows only tariffs or auction quotas as relief; requires adjustment plan |
| Trade Law Modernization Act of 1985 (H.R. 3777 and S. 1356) | Transfers president's authority to U.S. trade representative | Allows same options as under current law, but requires U.S. trade representative to consider adjustment plan |
| Trade Partnership Act of 1985 (H.R. 3522) | None, but transfers authority to determine relief from president to U.S. trade representative | Allows same options as under current law and gives U.S. trade representative option of interim relief |
| Administration proposal | None | Adds antitrust exemption to current options, provided no quotas |

reported out of the House Ways and Means Committee in May 1986 and passed by the full House that same month.

The proposals seeking to modify the escape clause, summarized in table 4-1 and discussed at various points throughout this chapter, are of two basic types. Some are designed to make the trade laws a better instrument for preventing injury from import competition by making temporary protection easier to obtain. Others seek to make the escape clause a more effective mechanism for restoring the competitiveness of import-damaged firms by using the trade laws to implement an industrial policy for declining industries. Such a policy would require companies hard hit by imports to comply with adjustment plans as a condition for receiving relief.

We believe these various initiatives are misguided. Quotas established by Congress for specific American industries hurt by trade are an inappropriate, inefficient, and ineffective response to their problems. Protection of certain sectors would have little favorable impact on unemployment or the overall trade deficit. And protection would save relatively few existing jobs at great consumer expense.

The proposals to amend the escape clause would also be counter-productive. Liberalizing access to relief would result in excessive protection, increasing prices on an unnecessarily broad range of products, and raising the risks of harmful retaliation by affected exporting nations. Meanwhile, those proposals that would impose conditions for obtaining relief, the so-called conditionality proposals, ignore the complexities of the adjustment process facing troubled industries, complexities that make industrywide planning and adjustment strategies undesirable in principle and beyond the capacity of governments to implement in practice. These proposals presume that government involvement in adjustment programs can speed the process of change and ensure that protection is temporary. As implemented in the American political environment, however, such plans are more likely to retard adjustment and to embroil the government in maintaining permanent protection. Indeed, the recent reinvestment requirements imposed on the steel industry by Congress highlight the great danger that adjustment plans would systematically encourage excess investment in industries that more realistically should shrink. More ominously, where shrinkage is called for by the plans, the conditionality mechanism would encourage the formation of cartels among trade-sensitive firms, which would inevitably impose permanent and unnecessary costs on consumers.

A much better approach exists for changing the existing escape clause mechanism. It lies in accepting the clause for what it is—a shock absorber for domestic protectionist pressures rather than an instrument of permanent protection or national industrial policy—but nevertheless seeks to make the temporary relief policy more cost effective. Our proposals for accomplishing this objective are outlined in the next chapter.


## Protecting Trade-Damaged Industries

The bill to impose quotas on imported textiles illustrates the dangers of leaving adjustment policy in congressional hands. As a report by the

Congressional Budget Office has made clear, advocates of textile quotas misdiagnose the problems and prospects faced by the American apparel and textile industries.[2] Proponents claimed that a surge in imports was the primary source of the erosion in employment in both industries, yet they failed to acknowledge the substantial role played by automation and the slow growth in demand or to distinguish between developments in the apparel and the textile industries. By building a coalition between groups who may well have deserved some temporary relief and groups who could obtain protection simply because they made a product labeled "textiles," proponents crafted a bill that magnified political clout at the expense of consumer welfare.

In testimony advocating the passage of legislation establishing textile quotas, Congressman Ed Jenkins (D-Ga.) relied on a study undertaken by Data Resources, Inc., for Burlington Industries analyzing the implications of failing to tighten restrictions on U.S. imports of textiles and apparel. Specifically, Jenkins claimed that imports of textiles into the United States had exceeded volumes allowed under the Multifiber Arrangement (MFA). Furthermore, the Data Resources study assumed that the recent 15 percent annual growth rate in textile imports would continue for the rest of the decade. In fact, however, the report by the Congressional Budget Office conclusively documented that the rapid growth in textile imports between 1980 and 1984 was possible only because imports before 1980 had grown at a rate below that allowed by the MFA. Accordingly, continued import growth at the annual rate of 15 percent assumed in the Data Resources projections is unsustainable, given that textile imports have reached their MFA ceilings. In addition, the Data Resources simulations assumed that once displaced, workers from the textile industry remain permanently unemployed. Yet according to a survey performed by the Department of Labor, 60 percent of the workers in the textile sector and more than 60 percent of the apparel workers displaced between 1979 and 1983 had found other employment by January 1984. Moreover, the median weekly earnings of reemployed workers who had been displaced from textile mills were 3 percent higher than in their previous jobs, while former apparel workers experienced a loss of only about 2.5 percent.[3]

That legislation limiting textile imports has been adopted by Congress

2. Congressional Budget Office, "Protecting the Textile and Apparel Industries" (CBO, September 1985).
3. Paul O. Flaim and Ellen Sehgal, "Displaced Workers of 1979–83: How Well Have They Fared?" *Monthly Labor Review*, vol. 108 (June 1985), pp. 3–16.

in the face of such contrary evidence highlights the influence of arguments favoring protectionist policies for certain industries. The justifications are of three types: that such measures will improve the trade deficit, that they will save jobs, and that they will help restore the competitiveness of domestic industries. Each of these purported rationales for sectoral protection, however, is flawed.

### Improving the Trade Deficit

The balance of trade in goods and services—the current account balance—is defined as the difference between exports and imports of goods and services. But the current account balance also reflects the difference between what the nation earns and what it spends. If the current account is in deficit, national spending exceeds national earnings from production and investments abroad. Net imports make up the difference.

Viewing the current account balance as a function of national spending behavior is crucial for evaluating claims that protecting industries can reduce the trade deficit. Consider an economy whose resources are fully employed or, alternatively, whose unemployment level remains constant. A quota levied on imports will raise spending on domestic goods in this economy. Given constant employment, imports must increase to meet increased demand, or else resources must be drawn from other sectors of the economy, thus reducing exports. Just as squeezing a balloon will redistribute but not reduce the total amount of air in the balloon, so, in the absence of a change in total national spending, imposing quotas will only change the composition of trade. Quotas will not affect the overall current account balance.

To be sure, in an economy with variable unemployment, selective protectionist policies could raise production and income in specific sectors in the short run without reducing them in other sectors. Provided that some of the increased income is not spent, the current account balance would improve. The critical question, however, is whether the economy's total production, typically constrained by the amount of monetary growth the Federal Reserve will allow, would also increase. Unless the Federal Reserve accommodates a rise in domestic production, employment in industries competing with imports will simply increase at the expense of employment elsewhere. Expanded production of one product thus again entails decreased production of another.

Movements in the exchange rate provide one mechanism by which this process operates. In the short run, a quota may reduce imports, but if other factors remain unchanged, it will also increase the current account balance, strengthen the currency, and thereby make it more difficult for other sectors in the economy to compete internationally. Protecting such industries as steel and textiles, for example, will keep the dollar strong and consequently hurt export sectors such as computers and aircraft. For the medium and long term, in which the economy tends toward a given employment level, quotas are unlikely to have major effects on the trade balance unless policies are adopted to shift national spending patterns.

The current account balance (exports minus imports) equals the sum of net private saving (saving minus investment) and government saving (tax revenues minus government spending).[4] The only way to improve the current account balance on a sustainable basis is to increase the sum of net private and government saving. This improvement can be accomplished by increasing tax revenues or gross private saving, or by reducing government expenditures or private investment. Quotas may have temporary effects on each of these variables but will not lead to a permanent improvement in the trade balance without permanent shifts in economywide saving and investment behavior.

Figure 4-1 shows what has happened to each of the influences on the current account balance since 1977. Significantly, the balance began to turn negative as the total government deficit (dissaving) increased. The current account balance has deteriorated most sharply since 1982, when net private saving dropped precipitously and the total government deficit began to exceed 3 percent of GNP.

4. This conclusion can be demonstrated from the accounting equality between the gross national product ($GNP$) and gross national income ($GNI$). $GNP$ is the sum of private consumption ($C$), private investment ($I$), government spending ($G$), and exports of goods and services ($X$), minus imports of goods and services ($M$), or

$$GNP = C + I + G + X - M.$$

$GNI$ equals the sum of private consumption ($C$), private saving ($S$), and government tax revenues ($T$), or

$$GNI = C + S + T.$$

Since $GNP$ must equal $GNI$, the two identities can be set equal to each other:

$$C + S + T = C + I + G + X - M.$$

After subtracting $C$ from each side, these terms can be rearranged into a fundamental identity:

$$(S - I) + (T - G) = X - M.$$

Figure 4-1. *Savings and Current Account Balance as a Percentage of GNP, 1977–85*

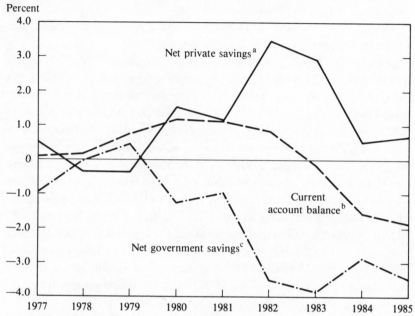

Percent

Source: Robert Z. Lawrence and Robert E. Litan, "Living with the Trade Deficit: Adjustment Strategies to Preserve Free Trade," *Brookings Review*, vol. 4 (Fall 1985), p. 7.
a. Gross private saving minus gross private investment as percentage of GNP.
b. Exports minus imports (goods and services) as a percentage of GNP.
c. Total revenues minus expenditures of all governments (federal, state, and local) as a percentage of GNP.

## Saving Jobs and Increasing Employment

Claims that protecting certain sectors of the economy will increase overall domestic employment are also questionable. Protection may add to jobs within an industry, but it will also raise prices of the goods or services produced in that industry. Increased prices may lead to fewer jobs for those distributing protected goods and for those using such products as intermediate inputs. An analysis of the quota bill undertaken on behalf of textile importers by the International Business and Economic Research Corporation, for example, estimates that while the quotas on foreign textiles would add about 71,000 jobs in the textile and apparel industries, these savings would be almost offset by declines in employment in the retail sector.[5] Protection of a linkage industry produces

5. Laura Megna Baughman and Thomas Emrich, "Analysis of the Impact on Textile

similar effects. By increasing domestic prices for steel, for example, quota protection undermines the competitiveness of the automobile and machinery industries, heavy users of steel.

Of course, proponents of protection have a narrower objective, that of assisting workers in particular industries. Quotas are, however, a very expensive means of saving jobs because they raise prices paid by consumers on both the imported goods subject to quotas and the domestically produced goods with which they compete. Weidenbaum and Munger have estimated that protectionism cost American consumers $58.5 billion in 1980.[6] The costs for each job saved by protection in different industries were high: $74,155 because of quotas on television receivers, $77,714 from tariffs and quotas on footwear, $85,272 from tariffs and quotas on carbon steel, and $110,000 on account of the "trigger price" system on steel. According to Hufbauer and Rosen, the cost to consumers from protection has continued to be high, roughly $53 billion in 1984.[7] In 1985 the Congressional Budget Office concluded that the costs to consumers of the original textile quota legislation alone would have been between 2.25 and 60 times the benefits to apparel manufacturers and between 1 and 20 times the benefits to producers of textiles.[8]

As high as they are, these estimates of costs for each job saved actually exaggerate the efficacy of protectionist measures in achieving employment objectives. Proponents of protection are generally more interested in saving the particular jobs of those *currently employed* in an industry than in preserving industrywide employment in the aggregate. But saving specific jobs can rarely be achieved. A quota may prevent imports from entering the market, but it cannot halt dislocations from other sources. Protectionists tend to believe that by diverting demand to domestic firms, quotas will improve their profitability and prevent plant closures. An improvement in prospective profitability that makes

and Apparel Trade Enforcement Act of 1985" (Washington, D.C.: International Business and Economic Research Corp., June 1985).

6. Murray Weidenbaum and Michael C. Munger, "Protection at Any Price?" *Regulation*, vol. 7 (July–August 1983), p. 15.

7. Gary Clyde Hufbauer and Howard F. Rosen, *Trade Policy for Troubled Industries* (Washington, D.C.: Institute for International Economics, 1986), p. 5.

8. CBO, "Protecting the Textile and Apparel Industries," pp. 30–33. The textile quota bill would have rolled back current import levels by approximately 5 percent, increasing costs to consumers for apparel and textile products by an additional $4 billion to $8 billion a year. *Economic Report of the President, February 1986*, p. 118.

new investment viable, however, may induce a change in plant location or the purchase of more automated production machinery. To the extent that protection encourages such a response, it could increase dislocation and reduce existing employment.

Such increased dislocation and reductions in existing employment frequently occur when domestic industries are protected from import competition. Of sixteen American industries studied by Lawrence and DeMasi that have received some type of protection under the escape clause, only the bicycle industry expanded after it received protection.[9] And even in this one instance, protection failed to save many of the jobs that existed when it was initially granted. Although overall production and employment in the bicycle industry grew after protection was introduced in 1955, each of the three largest bicycle manufacturers closed plants and moved in the next five years.[10] Indeed, to the degree that protection encouraged these firms to undertake long-term expansion, it also encouraged them to reexamine their choice of location.[11]

Similarly, saving the jobs of textile workers in New England was one reason given for the entrance of the United States into the first of several multilateral restraint agreements in 1962. Overall employment in the American textile industry did increase by about 9 percent between 1961 and 1973, a development that some have argued demonstrates the success of protection. But the aggregate data mask the massive relocations that occurred during these years as firms reduced their labor costs by

9. Robert Z. Lawrence and Paula R. DeMasi, "Do Industries with a Self-Identified Loss of Comparative Advantage Ever Adjust?" in Gary C. Hufbauer and Howard F. Rosen, eds., *Domestic Adjustment and International Trade* (Washington, D.C.: Institute for International Economics, forthcoming).

10. The Huffy Corporation left its small plant in Dayton, Ohio, in 1956 for new headquarters in Celina, Ohio, because of the lack of space in its old location and the desire to escape the very tight Dayton labor market. In 1956 also the American Machine and Foundry Company closed its midwest operations and built a new factory in Little Rock, Arkansas. The second largest domestic company, Murray Ohio Manufacturing, moved its bicycle operation from Cleveland to Lawrenceburg, Tennessee. See U.S. International Trade Commission, *The Effectiveness of Escape Clause Relief in Promoting Adjustment to Import Competition: Investigation No. 332-115 under Section 332 of the Tariff Act of 1930*, USITC Publication 1229 (March 1982), pp. 43–57.

11. In the 1955 hearings for import relief before the Tariff Commission (later the ITC), a bicycle trade union successfully supported the petition for protection. However, of the four companies whose workers were represented by the union in collective bargaining, workers from two were laid off when their plants closed in the 1970s. Lawrence and DeMasi, "Do Industries . . . Adjust?" in Hufbauer and Rosen, eds., *Domestic Adjustment and International Trade*.

moving to the South and West. Between 1960 and 1970 textile employment in New England declined by 34 percent, while increasing by 19 percent in the South.[12] And despite relocation, the problems plaguing the industry remained. The United States began the 1960s responding to pleas from Northeastern textile workers for protection and ended the decade answering the same pleas from textile workers in the South and West.[13] Had the new entrants in the South not been enticed into the textile industry, greater import penetration could have been accommodated with no additional dislocation.

The most recent evidence that protection is incapable of preserving existing jobs is provided by the trend of plant closings in the American automobile industry. Despite the billions of dollars in profits generated by the voluntary restraint agreement with the Japanese on automobile exports to the United States, six American auto plants closed between 1980 and 1983; 20 percent of the fifty remaining plants in the United States and Canada may close by the early 1990s.[14]

Even if companies or plants do not migrate, protection can stimulate the substitution of capital for labor, which also reduces total employment in the protected sector. Indeed, reductions in employment caused by investment could exceed the number of jobs preserved because of protection.[15] Protection could also stimulate investment in the United States by foreign producers, which might create jobs but could increase competitive pressures and dislocation for domestically owned firms and their workers and cause a wasteful use of resources. For example, Japanese television manufacturers invested in production facilities in the United States after an orderly marketing agreement limited television imports in 1977. This investment placed increased competitive pressure on the few remaining domestically owned manufacturers of television

12. U.S. Department of Commerce, Bureau of Economic Analysis, *Regional Employment by Industry, 1940–1970* (Government Printing Office, 1975), pp. 2, 229, 408. Over the longer 1950–70 period, employment in textile mills in northern states declined by an even more substantial 59 percent. See David Avery and Gene D. Sullivan, "Changing Patterns: Reshaping the Southeastern Textile-Apparel Complex," *Federal Reserve Bank of Atlanta Economic Review*, vol. 70 (November 1985), p. 35.

13. Despite current claims by textile interests that they are being damaged by imports, the rate of return on equity in the textile industry has risen dramatically, from 8.5 percent in 1980 to 11.2 percent in 1984. *Economic Report of the President, February 1986*, p. 117.

14. "A Gathering Glut: Auto Industry Faces Era of Plant Closings Due to Overcapacity," *Wall Street Journal*, February 14, 1986.

15. Peter Isard, "Employment Impacts of Textile Imports and Investment: A Vintage-Capital Model," *American Economic Review*, vol. 63 (June 1973), pp. 402–16.

receivers. In 1972 only two of the seventeen firms producing televisions in the United States were Japanese-owned; by 1983 twelve of the seventeen firms were foreign-owned, of which eight were Japanese. And even though the production of color television sets in the United States has increased since the late 1970s, production hours in the industry dropped by 32 percent between 1977 and 1983.[16]

In short, the benefits of protection for saving or creating jobs are generally overstated. While protection may create jobs in the aggregate, individuals in a protected industry who are currently working may not actually be helped by import restrictions.

Meanwhile, estimates of the costs of protection are generally understated for two reasons. First, the estimates typically assume that home markets are competitive. However, a quota that strengthens a domestic monopoly or the market power held by a few dominant producers and encourages them to raise prices could lead to fewer domestic sales and consequent reductions in employment.[17] Indeed, the so-called crisis cartels to aid declining industries, such as those that have been used in Japan or in Germany (in the 1930s), create a similar problem. Allowing these cartels encourages and legitimizes collusion to raise domestic prices and boost profits.[18] Such actions may well aid owners but may actually reduce employment.

Second, the cost estimates typically ignore the effects of protection on the labor market. Wage levels in any industry depend on the strength of competition in the market for the final products of that industry. A quota that reduces competitive pressures from abroad will thus reduce the elasticity of demand for both final products and labor, encouraging higher union wages and reducing industrial employment.[19]

Quotas may also take the form of provisions requiring domestic

16. U.S. International Trade Commission, *Color Television Receivers from the Republic of Korea and Taiwan* (USITC, 1984), pp. A-4, A-8–A-9, A-14.

17. Thus while the voluntary export restraint on Japanese cars meant that Americans bought fewer cars from Japan, it also encouraged the domestic producers to raise prices so that fewer American cars may have been bought as well. See Robert C. Feenstra, "Voluntary Export Restraint in U.S. Autos, 1980–81: Quality, Employment, and Welfare Effects," in Robert E. Baldwin and Anne O. Krueger, eds., *The Structure and Evolution of Recent U.S. Trade Policy* (University of Chicago Press, 1984), pp. 35–66.

18. One of the flaws of a trade policy that imposes conditions on recipients of protection is that it, too, may encourage cartelization, particularly where the conditions call for shrinkage of industrywide capacity. See the discussion below.

19. See Colin Lawrence and Robert Z. Lawrence, "Manufacturing Wage Dispersion: An End Game Interpretation," *Brookings Papers on Economic Activity, 1:1985*, pp. 47–115.

industry to use domestic materials. These local content provisions also raise costs to consumers. As Grossman has pointed out, the increase in the output of domestic components generated by domestic content requirements can be more than offset by the decrease in demand for final goods.[20] Similarly, quotas can induce foreign suppliers to upgrade the quality of their products. The VRAs limiting imports of Japanese automobiles into the United States during the past five years were instrumental in inducing Japanese auto manufacturers to export more of their larger and more expensive models.[21] In principle, greater proportions of high-quality imports under protectionist measures could displace a greater value of domestic production than under free trade.[22]

One might conclude from this analysis that if policymakers really desire to save the jobs of currently employed workers, the only appropriate measure would be to subsidize employment directly, as several European countries have done. Yet in practice such subsidy programs may not succeed in saving jobs or even in limiting dislocation. Employment subsidies may inhibit dislocation when temporary shocks would otherwise cause firms to lay off workers. If the shock turns out to be permanent, however, workers would eventually lose their jobs when government coffers run dry. Historically, governments have tended to reach budgetary constraints that induce them to remove such subsidies suddenly. In the long run, therefore, jobs are not saved, and the effect of suddenly withdrawing subsidies from large numbers of workers whose jobs are no longer economically viable may lead to more dislocation than if the market had operated freely. The European experience does not suggest that less adjustment is required simply because it is delayed.[23]

20. Gene M. Grossman, "The Theory of Domestic Content Protection and Content Preference," *Quarterly Journal of Economics*, vol. 96 (November 1981), pp. 583–603.

21. "End Voluntary Trade Quotas," *New York Times*, December 26, 1984.

22. See, for example, Robert E. Baldwin, "The Changing Nature of U.S. Trade Policy since World War II," in Baldwin and Krueger, eds., *Structure and Evolution of Recent U.S. Trade Policy*, pp. 9–12; Rodney E. Falvey, "The Composition of Trade within Import-Restricted Product Categories," *Journal of Political Economy*, vol. 87 (October 1979), pp. 1105–14; and Gary J. Santoni and T. Norman Van Cott, "Import Quotas: The Quality Adjustment Problem," *Southern Economic Journal*, vol. 46 (April 1980), pp. 1206–11.

23. For estimates of the waste in keeping the Shelton Works, a steel firm in the United Kingdom, open too long, see Victoria Curzon Price, "Alternatives to Delayed Structural Adjustment in 'Workshop Europe,'" *World Economy*, vol. 3 (September 1980), pp. 206–08. Once the British government determined to restore the financial

Finally, foreign competition is only one cause of job loss. Broad macroeconomic trends, shifts in demand, and improvements in productivity typically prove far more important. Even a prohibitively high tariff or a quota allowing no imports of a given product cannot stem the loss of jobs from these causes. Imposing a quota may, for example, achieve a one-time gain (at great expense) by inducing the substitution of domestic for foreign products, but thereafter employment may continue to decline as improvements in output per employee exceed the growth of demand. As McKenzie and Smith have argued, "textile and apparel employment combined would have fallen substantially . . . during the 1973–1984 period even if there had been no textile imports at all."[24]

Protection is therefore an extremely costly, unpredictable, and inefficient device for saving existing jobs. Indeed, by encouraging relocation and automation, by strengthening domestic monopolies, and by raising production costs, it may actually reduce the number of jobs in particular industries. Direct employment subsidies are more effective in saving existing jobs and they make the costs transparent, but if they are used to maintain permanently unviable jobs, they may also increase dislocation in the long run.

## Restoring Competitiveness

It is frequently argued that quotas or tariffs give firms in a domestic industry breathing room to modernize and restructure by allowing them to earn higher profits. As we pointed out in chapter 2, this argument ignores the possibility that companies could borrow from capital markets. It also presumes that only existing management and owners of firms currently in business should be responsible for undertaking new investment. On occasion, however, ridden by inferior management or by debt from previous investment errors, existing firms may be ill suited to undertake new investments. Selling assets to more creditworthy owners rather than salvaging the returns on past investments may be the appropriate method for facilitating industrywide recovery.

---

viability of the firm, it had to eliminate the excess labor much more rapidly than might have occurred without initial government aid.

24. Richard B. McKenzie and Steven D. Smith, "The Loss of Textile and Apparel Jobs: The Relative Importance of Imports and Productivity," Working Paper 96 (Washington University, St. Louis, Center for the Study of American Business, January 1986), p. 3.

Significantly, protection may simply fail to promote modernization. When an industry producing a standardized product loses its comparative advantage, far more than the latest technology will be required to regain competitiveness. In fact the passage of time may accentuate the cost differential between domestic and foreign firms. Given the rapid international diffusion of technology, foreign competitors can easily emulate the efforts of firms in a domestic industry to modernize. In such cases the availability of protection as an option may divert the industry's attention away from shrinkage and toward efforts to maintain protective barriers.

Comparative rather than absolute advantage will determine the ultimate viability of an industry in global competition. Participants viewing the process from the perspective of a single industry may find it difficult to appreciate the importance of comparative advantage. Indeed, the preamble to the Jenkins textile quota bill itself notes that increases in textile imports and import penetration in the U.S. market have occurred despite productivity increases in the past ten years that have been more rapid than in the rest of the economy.[25] If the textile and apparel industries abroad experienced even more rapid productivity growth relative to other domestic industries in their countries, the American apparel and textile industries could have suffered an erosion in comparative advantage even though their productivity has been well above average.

To be sure, some industries have made strategic errors that in time could be corrected. For example, the two oil shocks in the 1970s dramatically shifted the structure of demand for automobiles in the United States toward small cars, a shift that American manufacturers were not able to anticipate. Yet even in these cases the impact of protection on modernization depends on the form of that modernization and whether it is viewed as permanent or temporary. As noted in chapter 2, when quantitative restrictions are applied on imports, protection is least likely to promote modernization and may well prove counterproductive. The VRAs on Japanese automobiles not only increased the profits of American auto manufacturers but also raised the profits of their major foreign competitors, which may have enabled these competitors to perpetuate if not widen their cost advantage over American producers. In addition, quotas or VRAs will most likely be imposed to

25. H.R. 1562. The preamble noted that productivity in textile mills increased between 1975 and 1985 at the average annual rate of 4.2 percent, as compared with the 1.9 percent growth of all manufacturing in the same period.

protect unionized industries in which protection is least likely to promote modernization. Long-term protection encourages unions to seek higher wages, which if granted can further undermine the competitiveness of the domestic industry. Various forms of protection accorded to the American steel industry during the 1970s appear to have had this effect.[26]

### Conflicting Goals

The theory of economic policy recognizes that achieving a given number of objectives usually requires at least that number of policy instruments. Only in unusual circumstances can a single policy achieve two goals. Protection, however, generally intends to accomplish at least two conflicting objectives: preventing injury to domestic industries and creating breathing room to enable them to reestablish their competitiveness. These goals conflict because aiding firms to restore competitiveness often requires displacement—plant relocations, automation, and reductions in capacity. Accordingly, successful adjustment may actually increase the injury to some members of an industry. In contrast, if protection prevents dislocation by retaining or attracting resources incompatible with the long-run viability of an industry, competitiveness will be eroded. Protection therefore not only constitutes an extremely imprecise method for limiting dislocation and for inducing modernization, but its two objectives are inherently contradictory.

Some lawmakers have recently suggested that this contradiction can be resolved by requiring recipients of protection to commit themselves to adjustment strategies agreed upon jointly by representatives of management, labor, and government. Proponents argue that protection would save jobs while the adjustment requirements would help restore the international competitiveness of import-damaged industries. As we discuss later in this chapter, however, adding conditionality as another policy instrument would almost certainly be counterproductive. In practice, imposing conditions in return for assistance would probably not improve the abilities of domestic industries to adapt to international competition. Moreover, conditionality would facilitate collusion among firms in import-damaged industries, a result inconsistent with the best interests of American consumers and ultimately damaging to the industries themselves.

26. Lawrence and Lawrence, "Manufacturing Wage Dispersion," pp. 75–76.

## Modifying the Escape Clause

Two contrasting kinds of amendments to the escape clause have received serious consideration in Congress. Not surprisingly, given the prevailing protectionist environment, one group seeks to liberalize access to relief under the provisions of the escape clause. These proposals would relax the legal test that domestic industries must satisfy to be considered eligible for temporary protection and would increase the likelihood that some relief will be awarded if the International Trade Commission determines that injury has occurred. Expanding the escape clause, of course, would conform to the protectionist model of trade policy that we described in chapter 2.

The second group of proposals would have the federal government assume a more active role in pursuing an industrial policy for declining industries. Supporters of these proposals claim that the current escape clause provisions cannot adequately restore the competitiveness of firms in import-damaged industries because such industries can obtain temporary relief without any promises that they will use the breathing room afforded by protection to become more efficient competitors. Proponents of this view commonly cite the example of the United States Steel Corporation, which used its scarce resources to diversify out of the steel business by purchasing Marathon Oil Company in 1980, after the Carter administration tightened its enforcement of the unfair trade practice laws in an effort to assist the domestic steel industry.[27]

In the rest of this chapter we outline why neither of these broad approaches to amending the provisions of the escape clause is appropriate.

### Relaxing the Causation Test

Certain lawmakers have advocated two ways of easing the eligibility criteria for temporary protection under the escape clause. The most widely discussed method would relax the causation test, making it easier for domestic industries to prove that an increase in imports has

27. In particular, the administration effectively tightened limitations on steel imports by adopting a "trigger price" system for initiating unfair trade practice complaints. See Robert W. Crandall, *The U.S. Steel Industry in Recurrent Crisis* (Brookings, 1981), p. 43.

caused them serious harm. The proposed Trade Law Modernization Act (H.R. 3777), for example, would eliminate the "substantiality" requirement in section 201 of the Trade Act of 1974 so that domestic industries would merely have to show that imports were a "cause" rather than a "substantial cause" of serious injury. The act would also amend the causation test to state that a decline in domestic demand resulting from recession should not prevent the International Trade Commission from affirming that an industry or company has been injured.[28] The latter suggestion implicitly intends to reverse the ITC's rejection in 1980 of the domestic auto industry's petition on the ground that the recession then prevailing was a more important cause of injury than were imports.

An alternative approach for easing current eligibility criteria would require domestic petitioners to show that imports have caused only "material injury" rather than "serious injury."[29] The antidumping and countervailing duty laws use the former test, which is less difficult for domestic parties to satisfy than the "serious injury" standard.

A common premise underlies each of these proposals: that the current legal standards are excessively strict, precluding deserving import-battered industries from eligibility for temporary assistance. In a certain sense, of course, this premise is true. The American escape clause standards, modeled to a significant degree on the GATT standards, have sought to restrict the number of industries receiving temporary relief. A nation such as the United States that remains committed to free trade, however, faces the critical challenge of striking a balance between two opposing dangers. On the one hand, if the standards for obtaining import-related remedies are too restrictive, the escape clause mechanism cannot serve as an effective shock absorber for protectionist pressures. On the other hand, if the eligibility criteria are too weak, any domestic industry that faces import competition may become eligible for temporary protection. At what point do the costs of granting protection to companies that are less and less affected by import competition outweigh the political and economic benefits of having an escape clause procedure?

This question cannot be answered with certainty, but there are sound reasons to believe that further relaxing the current eligibility criteria

28. For example, section 501 of the proposed act states that a "cause may be important even though other causes, such as a general economic recession, are of equal or greater importance."

29. S. 839, *Congressional Record*, daily edition (March 17, 1983), p. S2387.

would bring about a situation in which the social costs of the escape clause would exceed its social benefits.

As we have already emphasized, erecting even temporary barriers to import competition is a costly way of channeling assistance. Imports may account for only a small portion of an industry's layoffs or a decline in its profits. Yet a quota or tariff on competing foreign goods will raise the price on all products, domestic and foreign, and thus generate relief at a cost to consumers that is far out of proportion to the losses from import competition sustained by domestic industries. Accordingly, targeted assistance for trade-related injury can be cost effective only when imports are truly the major source of a domestic industry's troubles.

Relaxing the current legal standards for proving import-induced injury would violate this criterion. As we documented in chapter 3, since Congress last liberalized these standards in 1974, domestic petitioners have prevailed in nearly 60 percent of the escape clause cases they have brought to the ITC. At this current "success rate," the proportion of affirmative injury findings is at an upper threshold, since many section 201 petitions, like many private lawsuits, lack merit.

Supporters of proposals to weaken the causation standard nevertheless argue that the current U.S. provisions are more stringent than required by GATT Article XIX, which requires only a causal connection between increased imports and serious injury and not that "substantial" cause be established.[30] This argument, however, overlooks the fact that in another important respect the U.S. escape clause law already favors domestic interests more than Article XIX does. Specifically, in the Trade Act of 1974 Congress dropped the requirement that serious injury result from concessions under the GATT and instead allowed the ITC to affirm injury when a company merely shows a causal relationship between increased imports and serious injury. As a result, sections 201 through 203 of the Trade Act are, in fact, no longer technically an "escape clause" but simply a vehicle for domestic interests to obtain temporary protection. While having such a vehicle may be desirable, if already permissive legal standards are weakened even further, the costs of the temporary-protection device will be more likely to outweigh its benefits.

---

30. Although the removal of the "substantiality" element of the causation test in the Trade Act would not technically violate GATT Article XIX, downgrading the "serious injury" standard to one of "material injury" would be inconsistent with the GATT escape clause. Article XIX clearly states that temporary exceptions to trade liberalizations are allowed only when increased imports cause or threaten "serious" injury. See chapter 2.

The only suggestion for modifying the current causation standard in the American escape clause that may have some justification is the proposed clarification that an economic recession cannot by itself constitute a more important cause of an industry's demise than import competition. Allowing the effects of a recession to preclude an affirmative injury determination, as it did in the 1980 automobile case, leads to the paradoxical result that a domestic industry is less likely to receive temporary relief when it most needs relief and when lawmakers may be particularly susceptible to pressures for protectionist legislation. Thus, after losing its section 201 case in 1980, the auto industry (and the workers in it) brought sufficient pressure to bear on Congress that the Reagan administration felt compelled to negotiate one of the costliest import restraints ever—the VRA with Japan, which continues today.

Although an affirmative injury decision by the ITC in the 1980 case would also have allowed the president to impose some type of temporary relief for the auto industry, at least the protection then could have taken the form of tariffs instead of the "voluntary" quota accepted by Japan. A tariff would have been more transparent. It also would have proved more effective in prodding domestic auto manufacturers to take necessary steps toward revitalization, because it would not have insulated them from Japanese competition during the economic expansion beginning in 1983. Equally important, tariffs would have allowed the U.S. Treasury to reap roughly $2 billion to $4 billion a year during 1983 and 1984, revenues that instead went to Japanese auto manufacturers because of the quotalike effects of the export restrictions.[31] Finally, even if an affirmative section 201 decision in the automobile case had resulted in a formal quota or orderly marketing agreement, that protection by law would have been temporary. In contrast, it is uncertain whether the current VRA will end any time soon.

### Narrowing Presidential Discretion

The relatively low rate at which presidents have granted relief to industry petitioners who have won their cases at the ITC has understandably led to demands that some type of escape clause remedy be made automatic. These demands are legitimate, and chapter 5 outlines our recommendations for responding to them. Several of the trade proposals

31. Robert W. Crandall, "Assessing the Impacts of the Automobile Voluntary Export Restraints upon U.S. Automobile Prices," paper prepared for the 1985 annual meeting of the American Economic Association.

now before Congress that purport to address this problem, however, would at best be ineffective in responding to these concerns, and at worst counterproductive.

The least effective proposals would transfer authority for making relief decisions from the president to the U.S. trade representative. These proposals apparently assume that the trade representative would more likely grant relief than the president when the ITC reaches an affirmative injury decision.[32] The suggestions would probably not, however, yield the results their proponents foresee. The U.S. trade representative not only is appointed by and reports to the president but also serves in the president's executive office. He or she would no more act inconsistently with the president's wishes than the director of the Office of Management and Budget, who also serves in the executive office, would contradict the president's views in budget negotiations with Congress.

The proposed Trade Enhancement Act of 1985 (S. 1860) takes a different approach. It would mandate implementing the relief recommended by the ITC (or measures substantially equivalent to it) when the commission determines that an adjustment plan agreed on by labor and management is likely to enable domestic firms to be competitive by the end of the relief period.[33]

Although not explicitly justified as such, other initiatives would also have the effect of making ultimate relief more likely. Specifically, these proposals would require the trade representative to grant an interim or emergency remedy pending a final ITC ruling if petitioners can demonstrate that imports have significantly increased and threaten to cause "irreparable harm."[34] Although interim relief would terminate if the commission found that the domestic petitioners were not seriously injured by imports, in the case of a final affirmative injury ruling, such

32. See, for example, the Trade Partnership Act of 1985, H.R. 3522; the Trade Law Modernization Act, S. 1356 and H.R. 3777; and the Comprehensive Trade Policy Reform Act of 1986, H.R. 4750.

33. This proposal is discussed further below. There is an escape clause built into this "conditionality" procedure, however. The president would be allowed to impose a less expansive remedy than the one proposed by the ITC (including no relief at all) if Congress, under an accelerated process of consideration, gives its approval within sixty days. If Congress does not approve the president's alternative, the commission's recommended remedy would automatically become effective, provided the commission has also reached an affirmative adjustment determination.

34. See the Trade Law Modernization Act, H.R. 3777 and S. 1356, sec. 502; and the Trade Partnership Act of 1985, H.R. 3522, tit. 1, sec. 204.

protection would make it politically more difficult for the trade representative to reject the commission's recommendation for relief. In the political marketplace it is far easier to refrain from granting benefits to a particular constituency than to withdraw those benefits once they have been awarded.

In general, the proposals designed to strip or narrow the president's discretion to provide assistance run serious risks. Because the ITC decides on the basis of producer complaints, it ignores other concerns, notably the effect of protection on consumers. The statutory requirement that no more than half the ITC's six commissioners may come from the same political party does not insulate the commission from this danger, since attitudes toward trade tend to be blurred across political lines.[35] Indeed, the statutory authorization for the ITC itself creates a bias in favor of domestic producers in all types of trade complaints, because tie votes dictate an affirmative finding.

Entirely eliminating the president's discretion to provide relief would also pose particularly severe complications for the conduct of foreign relations. GATT Article XIX requires member countries that invoke the escape clause to provide compensation to affected exporting nations. Because the nature of compensation can vary and in particular can depend on the outcome of delicate negotiations between the executive, Congress, and private interests, section 202 of the Trade Act of 1974 has allowed the president to consider as one factor in his decision the "effect of import relief on the international economic interests of the United States." This consideration has enabled the president to balance the political and economic costs of compensation with any benefits of trade protection for import-damaged industries. The automatic implementation of any ITC relief recommendation would prevent the president from attempting to balance competing economic and foreign policy interests, and instead would effectively require both that protection be imposed and compensation be provided, thereby harming other sectors of the economy.

One possible compromise for meeting the concerns of those who believe the prospects for ultimate escape clause relief are uncertain would require the president to impose a *de minimis* tariff of perhaps 5

---

35. ITC commissioners are appointed by the president and confirmed by the Senate for nine-year terms. The chairman is appointed by the president and serves for a two-year term. No chairman may be of the same political party as the preceding chairman.

percent (ad valorem) following an affirmative injury finding by the ITC. As with other types of escape clause relief, the tariff would phase out over five years. The decision to grant relief above the minimal level would remain entirely within the president's discretion.

A *de minimis* tariff would allow both the president and Congress to claim that at least some relief is automatically available to successful escape clause petitioners, thereby blunting demands by domestic interests for VRAs or legislated protection. Indeed, the prospect of some type of certain remedy would make the process of applying for relief more attractive to domestic interests in the first instance, and would consequently help to exclude protectionist demands from the legislative arena altogether. Both benefits could be gained at relatively little cost, since this proposal would provide automatic protection in the form of a tariff rather than a quota, while the limited nature of the relief would trigger only mild obligations to compensate foreign exporters.

There are at least two drawbacks to an automatic *de minimis* tariff, however. First, it would expose the nation to the risk of excessive protection if commissioners sympathetic to domestic interests were to dominate the ITC. Second, and perhaps more seriously, any proposal to incorporate a minimal tariff into the escape clause provisions could be so modified during legislative deliberations that any final product would be unacceptably protectionist. In particular, during legislative debates some lawmakers would no doubt attempt to raise the minimal threshold to levels inconsistent with the spirit of the proposal.

Whether a minimal automatic tariff would be a desirable remedy ultimately requires a political rather than an economic judgment. If Congress kept the tariff level reasonably low, it could contain the social costs of entitling every industry that succeeded in proving injury to minimal relief. Such costs would be worth bearing if through the *de minimis* tariff Congress significantly decreased the likelihood that it would yield to pressures for protectionist legislation from industries failing to obtain relief through the escape clause process. We do not pretend to know how this cost-benefit calculus would actually turn out. But we do know that as the *de minimis* tariff threshold increases, the justification for adopting the concept grows progressively weaker.

### Mandating Adjustment

The use of managed intervention in cases of import injury seeks to rehabilitate entire industries in the same way that the bankruptcy laws facilitate the restructuring of failing firms. In a typical bankruptcy proceeding, creditors of a troubled firm often agree to accept writedowns and lower interest on their loans if managers, workers, and shareholders agree to certain concessions and to adhere to specific commitments designed to make the firm more competitive. Shareholders might agree, for instance, to forgo the right to receive dividends for a certain length of time, or management and labor might accept wage cuts.

The federal government adopted the bankruptcy model in its 1980 decision to save the Chrysler Corporation by guaranteeing $1.5 billion of that company's debt. In exchange for that guarantee, Congress and the Treasury Department insisted that Chrysler's shareholders, creditors, managers, and employees all make significant concessions.[36] A loan guarantee board composed of the secretary of the Treasury, the chairman of the Federal Reserve Board, and the comptroller general was created to monitor the company's compliance with these commitments.

Chrysler has, of course, since recovered from its brush with bankruptcy. Advocates of managed intervention in cases involving relief from import competition suggest that what the government accomplished for Chrysler it can do for entire industries if only it required them to meet specific commitments designed to restore their competitiveness.

Congress is now considering several proposals to incorporate conditions for providing relief under the provisions of the escape clause. Prominent vehicles for this approach are the proposed Trade Law Modernization Act (H.R. 3777), the Comprehensive Trade Policy Reform Act of 1986 (H.R. 4750), and the Trade Expansion Act of 1986 (S. 2033). Each would make industry acceptance of an adjustment plan an integral component in the decision to award relief. Specifically, these proposals would allow firms or workers that petition the ITC for relief from import competition to request the formation of an industry advisory group to assess the current problems in the industry and to develop a strategy for enhancing its competitiveness. Members of the advisory groups would include the U.S. trade representative and officials from the Department of Commerce as well as representatives of firms and workers in the affected industry. If the ITC finds that the industry has

36. For an excellent description of these concessions and the negotiations leading up to them, see Robert B. Reich, "Bailout: A Comparative Study in Law and Industrial Structure," *Yale Journal on Regulation*, vol. 2, no. 2 (1985), pp. 180–87. For a complete account of the Chrysler experience, see Robert B. Reich and John D. Donahue, *New Deals: The Chrysler Revival and the American System* (Times Books, 1985).

met the escape clause standards, either the U.S. trade representative (in H.R. 3777 and H.R. 4750) or the president (in S. 2033) would consider the assessment of problems and the proposed strategy to overcome them in deciding whether to grant relief. If relief were awarded, a review committee consisting of the secretaries of labor and commerce and the U.S. trade representative would monitor the industry's adherence to the adjustment plan. If the review committee and the ITC later determine that the industry has failed, for reasons not due to changed circumstances, to meet the commitments set forth in the plan, the trade representative (H.R. 3777) or the president (S. 2033) could modify or terminate relief.

The Trade Enhancement Act (S. 1860) provides an even stronger conditionality mechanism. This legislation would *require* the president to impose the relief recommended by the ITC when labor, management, and government representatives agree on an adjustment plan. The president would retain the discretion, however, to award relief if the ITC finds the adjustment plan inadequate. The president would also be permitted to terminate relief if he later determines that the industry is not adhering to the commitments it has made.

Despite its superficial appeal, applying conditions for granting escape clause relief in either advisory or mandatory versions contains severe flaws. These flaws stem from the mistaken assumption that because conditions are desirable and indeed necessary to restructure a bankrupt or troubled firm, the law should require them when extending temporary trade-related assistance for entire industries.

*The nature of adjustment in declining industries.* One of the difficulties of implementing detailed adjustment programs for entire industries stems from the complex and highly varied nature of the required adjustment process. This can be seen in the adjustment patterns of sixteen U.S. industries that have successfully petitioned the International Trade Commission for trade-related assistance.[37]

In some of the sixteen cases, abandoning the industry rather than modernizing it was clearly the appropriate means of adjustment. Some industries had been declining not so much because of imports but because of competition from cost-effective, domestically available substitutes. For example, from 1962 to 1973 and 1962 to 1974 the domestic carpet

37. The detailed results of this analysis are reported in Lawrence and DeMasi, "Do Industries . . . Adjust?" in Hufbauer and Rosen, eds., *Domestic Adjustment and International Trade.*

and sheet glass industries, respectively, received tariff protection. Yet despite relatively low shares of imports in the domestic consumption of Wilton and velvet carpets (12.2 percent in 1977) and sheet glass (31 percent in 1976), the number of firms producing these products declined significantly—from twenty-seven carpet manufacturers in 1961 to seven in 1981 and from fourteen sheet glass manufacturers in 1961 to one in 1983. These declines mostly resulted from the rise of domestic substitutes—tufted carpets and float glass. Similarly, competing forms of entertainment and the declining birth rate contributed to an overall decline in the U.S. demand for pianos, which received tariff protection from 1970 to 1974. In 1970, when the piano industry first obtained trade protection, imports accounted for only 10.3 percent of domestic consumption. Yet this industry, too, continued to contract. With the wisdom of hindsight it is easy to see that shrinkage of these industries was warranted, but during the adjustment period itself many industry members might have hoped that revitalization was possible.

Trade-impacted industries making undifferentiated products in which costs alone determine sales also suffered major declines. Despite the breathing room afforded by tariffs, industries making high-carbon ferrochromium and nuts, bolts, and screws simply lost their ability to compete against less expensive foreign products.

In other cases among the sixteen studied, however, domestic industries benefiting from assistance under the escape clause recovered. Yet even in these situations the adjustments occurred in such varied fashions that they would have been difficult for anyone in either the government or the private sector to have predicted. Considerable foreign investment helped transform the domestic television receiver industry, which was protected by an orderly marketing agreement between 1977 and 1982. Plant relocation provided the principal means of adjustment for the bicycle industry, the only one of the industries examined that expanded aggregate production and employment following escape clause protection (which was lifted in 1968). And three industries—ball bearings, protected by tariff from 1974 to 1978, nonrubber footwear, protected by an orderly marketing agreement from 1977 to 1981, and stainless steel flatware, protected by tariff-rate quota in 1958–67 and 1971–76—adjusted by narrowing their markets and producing a more select group of products.

The different patterns of adjustment present significant problems in implementing any policies that place greater emphasis on planning. On the one hand, just because an industry experiences competitive problems, one cannot conclude that exit must be desirable. On the other hand, the French socialist slogan, "there are no outmoded industries, only outmoded technologies," would be an equally poor guide to action. Propping up industries in which comparative advantage has declined or disappeared wastes scarce resources that can be used more productively in other activities.

Moreover, adjustment strategies pursued by different firms *within* trade-damaged industries have varied as much as the adjustment responses of the industries themselves. Some have remained in the particular industry but have moved out of labor-intensive activities, as flatware manufacturers did. Others have shifted to alternative activities that require similar know-how, as in the case of producers of float glass rather than sheet glass. These adjustment strategies, however, will neither work for nor be available to all firms in an industry. De la Torre studied adjustment in the apparel industry and, on the basis of an extensive set of case studies, concluded in a similar vein: "Our data show that efforts aimed at increasing or maintaining high [industry] productivity, while essential, were not sufficient conditions for successful [company] operations. At the core of the growth company strategies was a dedication of time and resources to their external environment, that is, their marketing and their product policies."[38]

In short, experience also suggests that recovery and survival require different strategic responses on the part of different firms. The conditionality approach, however, inappropriately treats entire industries as the units for adjustment.

Some nevertheless argue that imposing conditions for rescue is politically desirable and will help to ensure that protection remains temporary. Specifically, they claim that such programs can accelerate adjustment. They also believe that if an industry participates in designing the adjustment program, it will face greater difficulties in asking for further protection if the plan fails.

This optimistic view fails to recognize the infeasibility of developing sound adjustment programs on an industrywide basis. The view also takes insufficient account of the way in which an adjustment program would be implemented in our political system. As we discuss below, imposing conditions in return for providing relief from import competi-

38. José de la Torre, "Corporate Responses to Import Competition in the U.S. Apparel Industry" (Georgia State University, College of Business Administration, 1978).

tion is likely to be ineffective in promoting adjustment because it would systematically favor reinvestment, even in those industries in which comparative advantage has declined or been eliminated. And where the propensity for reinvestment does not exist, a government-supervised adjustment program would create incentives for firms in import-damaged industries to collude, to the detriment of consumers. In either event, trade conditionality would tend to hinder rather than to promote adjustment.

*The politics of conditionality and the misallocation of capital.* A major flaw in trade conditionality is that it would almost certainly lead to wasteful investment of scarce capital that could be more productively employed elsewhere in the economy. The typical adjustment plan for an import-injured industry would most likely look very different from the typical bankruptcy proceeding, in which creditors force management to cut expenses and to avoid making major spending commitments. Even temporary trade protection offers firms in the industry new capital in the form of higher prices, and hence higher profits, on all products sold. The prospect of receiving additional funds virtually ensures that the typical adjustment plan would require firms to make significant new investments in the lines of business that compete with imports. Requiring the participation of labor and government representatives in drawing up the plan all but guarantees this result. To secure the assent of labor to any plan, management representatives would almost certainly have to promise that their firms would commit substantial resources to modernizing and perhaps expanding their facilities, actions that would maintain or at least not significantly reduce current levels of employment. Perhaps more important, management representatives would surely come to recognize that to promise major new investments would be the best way to demonstrate to government officials and specifically the decision-maker responsible for approving relief that their industries are serious about restoring competitiveness. Indeed, the more substantial the promised reinvestment commitments, the better the chances would be that import protection would be awarded.

The strong bias that adjustment plans would most likely display toward stringent investment conditions would not be disturbing if the additional funds committed to import-damaged industries offered the most productive uses of the nation's scarce capital. But as we have noted, virtually every industry that has benefited from some type of import protection over the past three decades experienced a decline in production and employment after protection ceased, providing striking evidence that even with government assistance import-damaged industries tend to shrink rather than to revive. Clearly, therefore, requiring firms in these industries to increase significantly their investments in manufacturing products that compete with imports would divert capital from financing other, more productive activities in the economy.

Unfortunately, Congress has recently imposed reinvestment requirements on the steel industry that will almost certainly produce the kind of waste in resources that we believe would occur on a grander scale if Congress fundamentally altered the escape clause mechanism in the way proponents of conditionality envision. In 1984 the ITC determined that imports had seriously damaged domestic manufacturers of carbon steel products. Although President Reagan formally denied the industry relief, he promised to negotiate VRAs to limit the steel exports of several major steel-making nations.[39] Congress seized this opportunity to write into the Trade and Tariff Act of 1984 the requirement that as a condition for retaining the authority to enforce these VRAs, the president must certify each year that the domestic steel industry "taken as a whole" has reinvested "substantially all of its net cash flow" from carbon and alloy steel production to modernize that industry. To make such a finding, the 1984 legislation requires the president to determine that each of the major steel companies—identified by name in the congressional report accompanying the legislation—meets this reinvestment obligation.[40]

The mistake made by Congress in 1984 could not be more obvious. As Crandall has recently shown, the domestic firms making the largest investment commitments to the steel business over the past decade have

39. By the end of 1984, VRAs had in fact been negotiated with seven steel-supplying nations: Japan, Korea, Brazil, Mexico, Spain, Australia, and South Africa. Collectively, these countries supplied 30 percent of U.S. steel imports in 1984. All the agreements are to last five years. For a more complete description of recent U.S. efforts to limit steel imports, see Theresa Wetter, "Trade Policy Developments in the Steel Sector," *Journal of World Trade Law*, vol. 19 (September–October 1985), pp. 485–96.

40. Steel Import Stabilization Act of 1984, 19 U.S.C. 2253 (originally enacted as title 8 of the Trade and Tariff Act of 1984, 98 Stat. 2948, 3043). The major companies mentioned in the legislative report on the steel reinvestment provisions included U.S. Steel, Bethlehem Steel, National Steel, Inland Steel, Armco, Republic Steel, Rouge Steel, and Wheeling-Pittsburgh Steel. See *Steel Import Stabilization Act*, H. Rept. 98-1089, 98 Cong. 2 sess. (GPO, 1984), pp. 11–12. The 1984 legislation also separately required the president to find, as a condition to the continuation of any steel import restraints, that each of the major steel companies "with significant unemployment" had committed at least 1 percent of its net cash flow from steel activities to worker retraining.

in fact shown the poorest performances in the industry.[41] Granted that between 1975 and 1981 the stock market rewarded those companies that were most aggressive in their steel-related investments (measured by returns to shareholders) relative to firms pursuing more modest investment programs, by 1984 every domestic steel company that invested heavily before the 1981–82 recession, including Republic, Sharon, and Wheeling-Pittsburgh, had vanished because of bankruptcy or forced merger, or was close to bankruptcy. Not surprisingly, the returns for shareholders in these firms fell between 1981 and 1984, despite the general bull market prevailing in much of this period. The companies that were more modest in their steel investment decisions, such as Inland, National, and U.S. Steel, produced at least a small positive return for their shareholders.

In short, imposing conditions in return for trade relief is flawed because the approach would replace market judgments about the long-term viability and size of import-damaged industries with political judgments. As we argued in earlier chapters, one virtue of the American escape clause process as it has operated thus far is that it has allowed government to refrain from deciding whether industries as a whole should shrink or attempt to remain at their current size. Escape clause protection has been granted to give firms in trouble the temporary breathing room in which to make that choice themselves. Although in theory conditionality would allow the same freedom of choice, the recent reinvestment obligations imposed by Congress on the domestic steel industry demonstrate all too clearly that in practice imposing conditions would very likely induce firms in import-damaged industries to waste additional resources in activities in which the United States no longer possesses a comparative advantage.

*Dangers of cartelization.* Advocates of imposing conditions for trade relief may nevertheless contend that management and labor representatives from import-injured industries would generally recognize the need for retrenchment and therefore agree on investment commitments that would allow their industries *both* to modernize and to reduce capacity. Admittedly, such plans might sometimes be negotiated. But the very structure of the conditionality proposals ensures that a second

41. Robert W. Crandall, "Trade Protection and the 'Revitalization' of the Steel Industry," paper prepared for the 1985 annual meeting of the American Economic Association.

and largely unrecognized danger will then surface: the high and undesirable risks of cartelization or anticompetitive joint conduct.

The tripartite negotiation process itself would lay the foundation for collusion by repeatedly bringing together managers of competing firms to discuss strategies for improving the performance of their industry as a whole. In cases in which the participants agreed on plans that call for reductions in industrywide capacity, it is difficult to imagine that the representatives would refrain from discussing, either at the formal meetings or off the record, how to apportion these reductions among industry members, or in other words, how to share the domestic market. The antitrust laws strictly proscribe market-sharing agreements, of course, because such agreements facilitate restrictions on output and the charging of excessive prices, the twin evils the Sherman Antitrust Act was designed to prevent.

The conditionality mechanism would create incentives for anticompetitive collusion even when adjustment plans do not call for shrinking capacity. Indeed, plans that call for substantial new investment may provide the most hospitable settings for industrywide coordination. No firm undertakes new investment without having a reasonable expectation that the earnings generated by the investment will be sufficient to justify taking the risk. Escape clause relief gives firms in import-damaged industries that are considering investment to modernize or expand only the limited comfort that, at least during the temporary relief period, earnings will be higher than if imports were not penalized. Nevertheless, import protection will rarely suffice by itself to encourage domestic firms to make substantial investments. However, if firms in the industry can use the process of negotiating an adjustment plan to arrive at tacit (or even overt) understandings about prices with their domestic competitors, ostensibly excessive reinvestment requirements can begin to look more reasonable. Indeed, the higher the reinvestment obligations, the stronger the incentives for collusion.

Plans requiring industries to shed capacity provide incentives to collude in a different way. To ensure that industry members will take the adjustment plans seriously, the conditionality proposals generally would allow the president or the U.S. trade representative to withdraw import protection if he later finds that the industry has not complied with its adjustment plan. For an individual firm in an industry agreeing to reduce capacity, this trap door creates uncertainty that invites collusion. Consider, for example, a tariff granted under the escape clause that raises the price of a product manufactured by an import-damaged firm by 20 percent. The firm proceeds to make its investment and employment decisions on that basis. Suddenly, the company discovers that the president has removed the tariff well ahead of its expiration date because he found that other firms in the industry have not shed capacity or modernized in a fashion consistent with the industrywide adjustment plan. Clearly, each firm in this industry will come to realize that it can minimize the uncertainty surrounding the length of the relief period by building on its relationship with other firms to find ways of tacitly coordinating pricing, investment, and marketing activities. Only through joint action, tacit or explicit, can each firm be assured that the industry as a whole will continue to receive the benefits of escape clause protection for the duration of the relief period.

One of the conditionality proposals, embodied in the Trade Enhancement Act (S. 1860), at least recognizes that the adjustment mechanism will not work in the way its proponents envision unless industry members collude. Accordingly, this proposal would authorize the president to instruct the attorney general to exempt the participants in discussions of adjustment plans from the antitrust laws when the beneficial international competitive effect of joint action "outweighs any adverse competitive impact on the domestic market."[42] Few adjustment plans would properly satisfy this requirement, however. Unlike escape clause relief, which by law is temporary, cartels function or have adverse effects on competition for far longer periods. Given the chance to collude for even the five years allowed in a typical adjustment plan, industry members can develop ways to extend their arrangements through tacit signals or understandings after the exemption period expires. Undoing the coordination thereafter will likely be a task too difficult for antitrust enforcers.

Under certain circumstances an antitrust exemption for participation in adjustment plan discussions could even prove futile. Although an exemption procedure would immunize current joint activities from antitrust attack, in later years the participants could be subject to allegations of anticompetitive conduct that may be facilitated by market power gained during the adjustment plan discussions. It would take years of litigation for courts to distinguish what portion, if any, of the

42. Trade Enhancement Act, sec. 306. Hufbauer and Rosen also recognize the need for granting participants in the adjustment plan discussions a limited antitrust immunity. However, we disagree with them about the merits of establishing such a process. Hufbauer and Rosen, *Trade Policy for Troubled Industries*, chap. 5.

market power that some firms could hold had been obtained through the exempted adjustment plan process and what portion may have been gained through unlawful anticompetitive joint activity.[43] The legal uncertainties could be so great that some companies with highly conservative antitrust counsel could either simply refuse to engage in adjustment plan discussions or participate so as to ensure that the agreed-upon plans remain so vague that courts would not be able to construe them as joint agreements and thus as grounds for antitrust violations. Of course, generally stated plans would be virtually useless for the purposes the proponents of conditionality have in mind.

Adjustment plans would also be unlikely to help resuscitate industries with numerous firms and an unorganized work force, such as the textile and apparel industries. The less concentrated and unionized the industry, the less likely that the workers and managers chosen to participate in discussions of the adjustment plan would be representative of their industry. They would instead tend to represent the narrow interests of the specific firms that employ them. Perhaps more important, the less organized the industry, the lower the likelihood that any firm or its employees would have confidence that other firms and their employees would act consistently with the plan to ensure continuation of the escape clause relief initially awarded. As a result, rather than providing a predictable framework of assistance, the conditions in the escape clause mechanism would make relief for unconcentrated industries so uncertain as to render it and the associated adjustment plans of very little use.

Indeed, the absence of concentration and organization appears to have plagued Japan's efforts to downsize its textile industry. Despite government purchases of surplus spinning looms, required registration of existing spindles and looms, and the banning of unregistered equipment, new producers have continued to enter the industry. It has been noted that the estimated number of new illegal (unregistered) looms in production "almost exactly cancelled the effective subsidies to reduce capacity."[44] In short, adjustment plans are only suited for concentrated

43. Section 2 of the Sherman Act prohibits acts of monopolization and attempts to monopolize. A threshold inquiry in section 2 actions is whether the defendant in fact has a monopoly, and if so, whether that power was gained as a result of superior business "skill, foresight, and industry," or through anticompetitive conduct. *U.S.* v. *Alcoa Co. of America*, 148 F.2d 416, 431 (1945). An antitrust exemption for participation in adjustment plan discussions would add another factor to be assessed by courts in deciding the source of monopoly (or market) power of defendants in section 2 cases.

44. See Arthur T. Denzau, *Will an Industrial Policy Work for the United States?*

and unionized industries, and then only because the facility of collusion in those sectors allows firms and workers to have confidence that if they adhere to the conditions in the plan, others will too.

Japan, which established in 1978 a broad program to facilitate adjustment by industries in long-term decline, at least has recognized that rationalizations of capacity may require firms to collude. Under its Structurally Depressed Industries Law of 1978, the Japanese government allowed domestic industries that believed they were "structurally depressed" to petition to be so designated in return for direct aid, tax incentives, and research and development support, all geared to assist in shedding capacity.[45] The 1978 law required each depressed industry to draw up a plan for both shrinking capacity and improving its competitiveness. The plan was to be submitted and subjected to the approval of an advisory body of the Ministry of International Trade and Industry (MITI) that included representatives of labor, management, government, and academia. Collectively, these features of the 1978 industries law closely resemble the adjustment plan process that would be created if Congress adopted the conditionality amendments to the U.S. escape clause statute.

The Japanese program for structurally depressed industries recognized, however, that planned reductions in capacity could require coordination among firms. Accordingly, the 1978 law authorized MITI to recommend to Japan's Fair Trade Commission that depressed industries be organized into cartels.

Experience under the statute was mixed. On the one hand, thirteen

---

(Washington University, St. Louis, Center for the Study of American Business, September 1983).

45. According to the law, a structurally depressed industry is one that has excess capacity, projected long-term instability, and a need to reduce capacity. The law specifically cites the steel, aluminum, synthetic fiber, and shipbuilding industries as structurally depressed. Other industries may also receive the designation if two-thirds of their members so request. For general descriptions of the 1978 law and its 1983 amendments, see Margaret A. McGregor and Katherine V. Schinasi, "Positive Adjustment Policies toward Declining Industries in Japan," and Michael K. Young, "Structurally Depressed and Declining Industries in Japan: A Case Study in Minimally Intrusive Industrial Policy," both in *Japan's Economy and Trade with the United States*, prepared for the Subcommittee on Economic Goals and Intergovernmental Policy of the Joint Economic Committee, 99 Cong. 1 sess. (GPO, 1985), pp. 168–80, 181–98; Douglas P. Anderson, "Managing Retreat: Disinvestment Policy in the United States and Japan," in Thomas McCraw, ed., *America vs. Japan* (Harvard Business School Press, forthcoming); and Merton J. Peck, Richard J. Levin, and Akira Goto, "Picking Losers: Public Policy toward Declining Industries in Japan," Yale Working Paper (April 1986).

of the fourteen industries designated as structurally depressed achieved 90 percent of their planned capacity-reduction goals.[46] On the other hand, many of the firms in these industries would probably have achieved a similar degree of capacity reduction in the absence of the law, since only a small portion of the available government assistance was actually used. Perhaps more important, the manner in which capacity reduction actually occurred bore very little resemblance to the adjustment called for in the plans.[47] The latter finding, of course, reinforces the suspicion that American firms would have strong incentives to collude under a conditionality program. Only through joint action could industry members assure themselves that relief would not later be removed because of their industry's failure to adhere to the approved adjustment plan.

The Japanese themselves have recognized the limitations of their depressed industries statute, as well as the potential dangers it created for consumers by so freely authorizing the establishment of cartels. Accordingly, in 1983 they amended the Structurally Depressed Industries Law to give their Fair Trade Commission the power to review the ongoing operations of the cartels and, if appropriate, to recommend significant changes if the cartels are found to have an adverse effect on internal competition. The United States would do well to learn from the Japanese experience. Congress should recognize the high risks of cartelization created by conditionality mechanisms for entire industries and reject proposals that make conditionality an integral part of the process of granting assistance under the provisions of the escape clause.

46. McGregor and Schinasi, "Positive Adjustment Policies," in *Japan's Economy*, p. 174.

47. Young cited the case of the synthetic fiber industries in Japan. The firms agreed on a plan for capacity reduction, but equipment was scrapped by each in a manner far different from the guidelines established in the plan. Young, "Structurally Depressed and Declining Industries in Japan," pp. 188–89.

# CHAPTER FIVE

# Policy Recommendations

THE BEST FRAMEWORK for trade policy is one that seeks to achieve free trade but that also contains cost-effective safety valves for reducing protectionist pressures. In principle, both the escape clause and the trade adjustment assistance program can serve as these safety valves; in practice, both have defects. This chapter discusses how the flaws can be corrected.

## Improving the Escape Clause

The U.S. escape clause mechanism has a number of positive features. The provisions have restricted the availability of protection and generally kept it temporary. Emergency relief has usually taken the form of tariffs rather than more costly quantitative limitations. And the escape clause mechanism has helped diffuse political responsibility for trade policy, thereby diverting pressure for protectionist solutions from the politically charged legislative arena to the quasi-legal administrative forum offered by the International Trade Commission.

Recent events, however, have exposed fundamental weaknesses in both the American and GATT escape clauses. The U.S. provisions unwisely permit the president to award temporary relief by means of quotas and orderly marketing agreements as well as tariffs. The broad discretion in remedies allowed the president has also made petitioners who are successful before the ITC so uncertain of ultimately receiving any assistance that the escape clause mechanism is losing its ability to function effectively as a shock absorber for protectionist sentiment. The GATT escape clause, meanwhile, has become progressively less effective as member nations have turned to voluntary restraint agreements to circumvent the onerous nondiscrimination and compensation requirements imposed by Article XIX. Major reforms to convert quotas to tariffs, to discourage the use of VRAs, and to provide automatic relief for import-damaged firms and workers would correct these weaknesses.

### Tariffs Designated for Adjustment

Both the U.S. and GATT escape clause provisions should eliminate quotas or orderly marketing agreements as acceptable alternatives for providing assistance. If the U.S. escape clause authorizes any emergency protection, it should be only by tariffs set to decline over a five-year period. The ITC should also be required to present to the president and to the public an analysis of the economic effects of any tariff remedy it may recommend. This suggestion, which has been advanced by Baldwin, would make the social costs and the benefits of temporary tariffs fully transparent.[1] Such an evaluation is currently made by economists in the executive branch, most often in the president's own executive office. The analyses are not always released to the public, however. Routine publication of the ITC's analyses would not only assist the president in making his relief decision, but would add to the public record the findings of an independent agency charged with trade responsibilities.

We also believe that all existing quotas and OMAs should be converted to declining tariffs (although the phaseout period could extend beyond the five years allowed for escape clause relief).[2] Tariff revenues should be designated to fund a revised adjustment assistance program for trade-displaced workers and a new program for compensating exporting nations harmed by the conversion of quotas to tariffs.[3] Reserving these revenues is desirable to prevent their use for general reduction of the budget deficit.[4]

1. Robert E. Baldwin, "Rent-Seeking and Trade Policy: An Industry Approach," National Bureau of Economic Research Working Paper 1499 (Cambridge, Mass.: NBER, November 1984), p. 20. Baldwin notes that the ITC is already required to assess the economic impacts when the president decides to negotiate tariff reductions.

2. For a similar view see Gary Clyde Hufbauer and Howard F. Rosen, *Trade Policy for Troubled Industries* (Washington, D.C.: Institute for International Economics, 1986); and Gary Clyde Hufbauer and Jeffrey J. Schott, *Trading for Growth: The Next Round of Trade Negotiations* (Washington, D.C.: Institute for International Economics, 1985), pp. 16–17.

3. Our proposal to designate tariff revenues for trade assistance builds on and extends section 245 of the Trade Act of 1974, which reserved some funds from customs duties to retrain trade-displaced workers. However, the "adjustment assistance trust fund" called for in the act was never created. See James A. Dorn, "Trade Adjustment Assistance: A Case of Government Failure," *Cato Journal*, vol. 2 (Winter 1982), p. 872.

4. The Comprehensive Trade Policy Reform Act of 1986 (H.R. 4750), passed by the

However, the revenues from specific tariffs should not be used solely to fund the adjustment programs for workers displaced in the industries protected by these tariffs.[5] Tying the funding for adjustment to particular tariffs generates enormous pressure on the president to grant tariff relief every time the ITC decides that a domestic industry has been injured by imports. This pressure can be avoided by simply dedicating all tariff revenues to the fund to be used for adjustment assistance generally. Indeed, as we discuss below, the revenues from converting existing quotas to tariffs could alone conservatively cover the cost of our proposed adjustment efforts for at least a decade, which would eliminate the need for any new tariffs.

Most objections to our tariff-funded adjustment proposal can be easily addressed. For example, one frequently noted drawback to conventional tariffs is that fluctuations of exchange rates can offset or eliminate the benefits tariffs confer on domestic industries. An appreciation of the dollar by 20 percent, which may simply reduce the dollar price of imported goods by that amount, would offset the protective effect of an even larger tariff (25 percent).[6] However, expressing any declining tariff schedule in dollar-equivalent terms and adjusting the nominal tariff rates periodically (perhaps quarterly or monthly) to offset movements in exchange rates would avoid this result. Of course, depreciations of the dollar would have the opposite effect and would reduce the nominal tariff rate.[7]

Another potential problem is that converting existing quotas to tariffs would impose losses on exporting countries, particularly on those less developed. Whereas tariffs allow the governments of importing nations

---

House in May of 1986, incorporates this principle. It would permit import rights under any quota granted pursuant to the escape clause to be auctioned. The revenues generated from the auction, together with any revenues from tariffs implemented under the escape clause, would be placed in a trust fund for trade adjustment assistance.

5. This is suggested by Hufbauer and Rosen, *Trade Policy for Troubled Industries*, chap. 5.

6. Consider an imported item priced at $1.00 before a tariff of 25 percent is applied. A 20 percent dollar appreciation lowers the pretariff price of the item in the United States to $0.80; the tariff-inclusive price of the item is back to $1.00 ($0.80 × 1.25).

7. The maximum increase in tariffs allowed under the current escape clause law is 50 percent ad valorem. If this upper limit were not changed, it could in rare cases prevent any adjustment in the nominal tariff rate from fully reflecting changes in exchange rates. It might therefore be advisable to amend the tariff provisions to allow nominal tariffs exceeding 50 percent, but only when the excess over the ceiling is due entirely to exchange rate adjustments.

to reap directly the benefits of the higher prices generated by protection, quotas confer those benefits on exporting countries. As a result, exporting nations that would be adversely affected would strongly oppose any conversion of quotas into tariffs.

Establishing a trade adjustment assistance program for exporting countries analogous to the TAA for American workers displaced by trade could significantly mitigate this potential opposition. This compensation program could be funded by revenues earned from quota conversion. This conversion should be done in two phases to minimize both the adjustment costs and the initial uncertainty. In the first phase, global auction quotas would replace existing country quotas in order to set a tariff-equivalent price on existing protection; in the second, self-liquidating tariffs would replace the auction quotas.[8]

We can best illustrate this compensation mechanism by showing how it could permit dismantling the current Multifiber Arrangement, which has governed textile and apparel trade among most major textile-producing and consumer nations since 1974 but expires in August 1986.[9] Initially, the United States (and other countries currently covered by the MFA) could aggregate the existing quotas and auction them to the highest bidders. In this phase, which could last for perhaps three years, the domestic textile and apparel industries in each importing nation would therefore receive precisely the same amount of protection that they currently receive under the MFA. This is because the auctioning of quota rights would not disturb the quota allocations themselves. However, shifts would occur in the shares enjoyed by the various textile exporters. Highly competitive exporters would gain shares; less competitive exporters would lose. This contrasts with the current quota system, which locks in textile-exporting countries to specific shares regardless of the competitiveness of their producers.

During this initial phase the governments of importing countries (in

8. It is sometimes assumed that auction quotas and tariffs are equivalent. For example, the omnibus trade proposal (S. 2033) introduced by Senator Lawton Chiles (D-Fla.) would eliminate quotas and orderly marketing agreements as relief alternatives under the escape clause but permit both tariffs and auction quotas. While both tariffs and auction quotas yield revenue for the government (unlike strict quotas), the two remedies do not have identical effects. Auction quotas still prohibit entry of imports above the quota ceiling. In contrast, tariffs allow marginal imports, but with a price penalty equivalent to the tariff.

9. For a recent discussion of proposals to dismantle the MFA, see Martin Wolf, "How to Unravel the Multi-fibre Arrangement," *World Economy*, vol. 8 (September 1985), pp. 235–48.

this case the United States) could rebate some proportion of the revenues received from the quota auctions. Indeed, estimates presented later in this chapter show that at least half these revenues—in excess of $1 billion for the first three years—could be rebated, leaving sufficient monies to fund a generous trade adjustment program for trade-displaced American workers. The governments could distribute the rebates to exporting nations in rough proportion to their existing market shares. During the initial phase, therefore, textile and apparel production among exporting countries would shift toward efficient producers, while less efficient firms and their workers would benefit from compensation.

Allowing the market to set tariff-equivalent values of existing quota rights would enable the conversion phase of the program to proceed. Tariffs would first be set at levels determined by the price of the auctioned quotas. Thereafter they could be phased out over a period as long as fifteen years. The least developed of the exporting nations could continue to receive declining rebates during this extended period.

This system for dismantling the MFA that we have outlined would allow the textile sector to be reintegrated into the rules of the global trading system. The first phase would confer the benefits of nondiscrimination and of entry determined by efficiency rather than historical precedent; the second would establish a market-oriented system of tariffs. A final phase would result in free trade. A long phase-in period would allow existing investments to be amortized gradually while minimizing uncertainty.

### Discouraging VRAs

The negotiation of voluntary restraint agreements would, of course, circumvent our "tariff only" prescription for escape clause relief. Although it is unlikely that VRAs can be outlawed—by definition they are "voluntary"—it should be possible to erect some roadblocks that would deter the executive branch from requesting other nations to establish export restrictions.

At a minimum, Congress should direct the Customs Service to use no monies to monitor or assist in enforcing other nations' attempts to impose VRAs.[10] Such an action would allow exporters in other countries to

10. The Steel Import Stabilization Act of 1984, for example, gives the Customs Service the authority to enforce restrictions on exports to the United States of steel pipes and tubes from the European Economic Community nations, in accordance with the U.S.-EEC arrangements on pipes and tubes of 1982.

undermine the VRA, either by using third countries as conduits for exporting goods to the United States or by diverting production into similar items not covered by the restraint agreements.[11]

A more ambitious method of deterring the use of VRAs would be to extend the reach of the 1890 Sherman Antitrust Act, which proscribes joint action by competing firms, to cover foreign participants in the export cartels that are routinely formed to help enforce voluntary export restrictions adopted by other countries.[12] Although foreign participants in export cartels may be sued in this country if they or their subsidiaries do business here, U.S. authorities have, as a practical matter, exempted them from prosecution under the doctrine of "sovereign compulsion," on the theory that foreign governments mandate joint conduct among their exporters. Congress could amend the Sherman Act to provide that, in the absence of clear and convincing evidence demonstrating that a foreign government has specifically directed its exporters to collude, the members of any cartel or joint arrangement restricting exports to the United States could not defend themselves by invoking a defense of sovereign compulsion. An even bolder amendment would simply bar foreign firms that are proved to have participated in an export cartel from using sovereign compulsion as a defense. Although either of these proposed changes to the antitrust laws would run counter to the current concern that American antitrust laws are too liberally applied to foreign residents, there is a strong case for extending the reach of the Sherman Act to foreign cartels, even those that may be blessed by their own governments, whose activities clearly have the effect of raising prices of goods sold to American consumers.

Similarly, Article XIX should be amended in order to discourage the widespread evasion of GATT rules by means of VRAs. The compensation requirement should be suspended under two carefully circumscribed conditions: when member countries establish quasi-legal procedures for determining whether domestic industries are entitled to temporary relief under Article XIX (or equivalent standards) and when the form of relief is limited to declining and nondiscriminatory tariffs rather than quotas,

11. The 1982 restraint agreements governing steel trade between the United States and the European Economic Community contained a "diversion clause" designed to prevent European steel producers from avoiding the export limits by shipping steel products to the United States that were not explicitly covered by the agreements.

12. See Jan Tumlir, *Protectionism: Trade Policy in Democratic Societies* (Washington, D.C.: American Enterprise Institute for Public Policy Research, 1985), pp. 48–50.

orderly marketing agreements, or any other type of quantitative restriction. The first criterion guarantees that the government decisionmaking process will be transparent and that both importing and foreign exporting interests will have a fair chance to present their cases before national authorities reach an injury determination. The second requirement ensures that any protection granted will not severely distort international trade. Under our proposal, the GATT secretariat would determine whether nations adhere to these criteria, and if they do, would exempt them from providing compensation when they invoke Article XIX.[13]

Admittedly, these suggestions for reforming Article XIX would not eliminate all reasons for circumventing it. Some nations might continue to raise trade barriers on a discriminatory basis, a practice outlawed by the GATT (the United States and the EEC nations, for example, have negotiated VRAs limiting exports only from Japan and other Asian countries). It would also be unrealistic to expect the signatories to the various bilateral agreements negotiated under the auspices of the Multifiber Arrangement to abandon overnight the longstanding systems of quotas on textiles and clothing in favor of converting them to tariffs. Nor would it be realistic to expect the signatories to use only "temporary" import protection measures under Article XIX. Nevertheless, removing the compensation requirement under the carefully circumscribed conditions we have outlined would go a long way toward restoring Article XIX to a meaningful place in the multilateral system of trading rules.

### Automatic Relief for Escape Clause Winners

As we argued in chapter 4, current concerns about the uncertainty of relief under the American escape clause mechanism are not best addressed by requiring that the ITC's relief recommendations always be implemented. Instead two remedies that are more cost effective than tariffs should automatically be granted for industries that prove import-induced injury to the ITC, while preserving the right of the president to determine in any given case whether tariffs should be awarded as a form of supplemental relief. First, workers in an affected industry who lose their jobs in the years following a positive escape clause finding by the

13. Similar suggestions have been advanced in John H. Jackson, "The Role of GATT in Monitoring Safeguards and Promoting Adjustment," in Gary Clyde Hufbauer and Howard F. Rosen, eds., *Domestic Adjustment and International Trade* (Washington, D.C.: Institute for International Economics, forthcoming); and Hufbauer and Schott, *Trading for Growth*, p. 45.

ITC should receive benefits under a new trade adjustment assistance program, described below, that would promote rather than delay their adjustment.[14] Second, firms in industries found by the ITC to be damaged by imports that wanted to merge should be judged under somewhat relaxed antitrust standards, provided they did not also benefit from quantitative restrictions on competing imports. The automatic triggering of both these measures would make it much easier for lawmakers to fend off requests for protectionist legislation by import-injured industries that fail to obtain other relief.

*Automatic trade adjustment assistance.* Under current law the ITC cannot recommend that the president award both adjustment assistance to displaced workers and import protection for a domestic industry. Indeed, neither the ITC nor the president determines whether adjustment assistance is to be given. Instead, the president may merely order the Department of Labor to expedite consideration of requests for TAA benefits, which are then paid only to groups of workers within industries and firms able to prove that imports constitute a substantial cause of their layoffs.

Our proposal would channel TAA benefits automatically to all displaced workers in an industry that the ITC determines to be seriously injured by import competition. Although this automatic payment system would expand the class of potential beneficiaries relative to earlier TAA programs, a broader assistance program is justified. It would speed the payment of benefits, since affected workers would not need to obtain separate and duplicative certification of import-induced injury from the Department of Labor, and it would provide reemployment incentives to a larger number of displaced workers. Rather than paying those workers only as long as they remain unemployed—the method of compensation used in the TAA program since 1981—our proposed system of trade adjustment assistance would encourage readjustment by making additional trade-related compensation available when displaced workers find alternative employment. A combination of revenues earned by converting all existing quotas to declining tariffs and any monies generated by new tariffs could finance the program.

Our proposed plan would eliminate the component of TAA that has provided direct financial assistance to specific firms, but this part of the

14. Our proposal would continue to allow groups of workers to apply directly to the Labor Department for TAA benefits without going through the escape clause process at the ITC. See the discussion below.

current program has never been significant and has channeled funds to the least efficient producers in trade-damaged industries. We also reject the proposal, recently advanced by Hufbauer and Rosen, to subsidize firms in import-damaged industries to help them retire capacity.[15] While the evidence we have surveyed suggests that reducing capacity is generally an appropriate response for industries battered by import competition, it would be unwise for government to assume in every case that capacity should shrink. The proposal to subsidize capacity reductions also poses severe administrative complexities because it would require the federal government to audit the production capacities of individual firms, a task it has never undertaken.

*Relaxed merger standards.* In addition to providing automatic trade adjustment assistance, the American escape clause mechanism would be improved if merger standards were automatically relaxed for industries found to be suffering serious injury from imports, unless the industries were also shielded from foreign competition by quotas, OMAs, or VRAs.[16] Our merger proposal would not violate traditional antitrust principles; indeed, it would be consistent with them. At the same time, because the relaxed merger treatment would be available automatically, it would blunt the force of demands for legislated protection by domestic industries to whom the president denies tariff protection. Lawmakers would be able to point to the relaxed standards, as well as automatic trade adjustment assistance, as concrete reasons for refusing to enact highly costly and potentially long-lasting forms of quantitative import limitations. Less restrictive antitrust standards for mergers might also be sufficiently important to some firms to persuade them not to lobby for legislated trade barriers.

These political and economic factors provide a sounder basis for relaxing merger standards than the possibility that a more liberal merger policy would promote efficiency-enhancing rationalizations of capacity. To a limited degree a policy facilitating mergers would prove attractive to firms reluctant to shed too much capacity (because they hope that

15. Hufbauer and Rosen, *Trade Policy for Troubled Industries*, p. 84.
16. A relaxed merger standard could be applied, however, if the domestic industry were protected by a tariff. With a tariff, even a firm with a substantial share of the domestic market that attempts to raise prices faces the prospect that foreign suppliers will increase their shipments to the market and thereby defeat or reduce the gains from the attempt. The same firm, however, would be free to exercise any power it has over prices in the domestic market if the industry in which it competes were protected by a quota.

106                                                SAVING FREE TRADE

their domestic competitors will shut down or significantly scale back
production first), but that are deterred from undertaking lengthy merger
negotiations by the uncertainty of response by federal antitrust agencies.
For such firms the near certainty of a green light from the antitrust
authorities would be an added inducement for proceeding through the
escape clause process rather than pressing Congress for protection. The
potential gains in efficiency from a relaxed merger policy for import-
damaged industries should not, however, be overstated. The evidence that mergers in declining industries generally have provided an
effective means of encouraging the rationalization of capacity is at best
ambiguous.[17]

Nevertheless, there are two ways in which the merger standards set
forth in section 7 of the Clayton Act could be relaxed in the context of
appeals for relief under the provisions of the escape clause. Section 7
could be amended to build in the basic modes of analysis reflected in the
1984 merger guidelines announced by the Department of Justice and the
Federal Trade Commission,[18] but to liberalize their application when
weighing the antitrust consequences of mergers between firms in import-
damaged industries. A second amendment, favored by the Reagan
administration, would relax the standards themselves for mergers involving firms in import-damaged industries. A brief review of how the
antitrust implications of horizontal mergers—those involving competitors—are typically assessed by the federal antitrust enforcement agencies will best explain both approaches.

Section 7 of the Clayton Act prohibits mergers whose effect *"may be
substantially to lessen competition, or to tend to create a monopoly"* in
any line of commerce in any section of the country.[19] Since 1968 the
Department of Justice and the Federal Trade Commission have used
somewhat mechanical guidelines, based on judicial decisions, to determine whether a horizontal merger should be challenged in court under
this standard. The guidelines are based on the premise that mergers in
structurally concentrated industries—those in which a relatively small

17. See Mark W. Frankena and Paul A. Pautler, *Antitrust Policy for Declining
Industries* (Federal Trade Commission, Bureau of Economics, October 1985), pp. 31–61.
18. "U.S. Department of Justice Merger Guidelines" (June 14, 1984); and Federal
Trade Commission, "Statement Concerning Horizontal Mergers" (June 14, 1984). These
two documents set forth similar enforcement guidelines. The Justice Department's 1984
guidelines updated and elaborated its 1982 merger guidelines (issued June 14, 1982).
19. 15 U.S.C. 18 (emphasis added).

number of firms make most of the sales—are most likely to result in the anticompetitive conditions the Clayton Act was designed to prevent.[20]

For present purposes the most important new feature of the 1984 merger guidelines is the way in which they define relevant product and geographic markets, since this definition affects how foreign competition is counted in assessing the effects of mergers involving import-sensitive firms.[21] In the past, courts have taken a relatively restrictive approach to market definition and particularly to the weight given foreign competition. Broadly speaking, geographic markets have been defined on the basis of current consumption and shipment patterns. As a result, while some courts have acknowledged that foreign production could be counted under certain circumstances in computing the market shares of domestic competitors, most courts have been reluctant to do so.[22]

The 1984 merger guidelines take a much more expansive approach toward defining relevant markets, because they consider both existing and potential competition. For this purpose, the guidelines begin with

20. The new merger guidelines have changed the method of computing market concentration. Under the new procedure, concentration is to be computed by taking account of the share of all firms in a market but giving disproportionate weight to the leading firms, rather than only on the basis of the share held by the top four or eight producers, as was the case under the 1968 guidelines. The new guidelines implement this through the Herfindahl-Hirschman index (HHI), which is computed as the sum of the squares of the market shares of each firm in a market, expressed in absolute percentages. For example, the HHI of a four-firm market where the competitors have 40, 30, 20, and 10 percent shares respectively is 3000 (1600 + 900 + 400 + 100). The new guidelines note that an antitrust challenge is most likely when a proposed merger would increase the HHI by more than 50 points in an industry where the premerger HHI exceeds 1800.

21. Of potential significance, the 1984 merger guidelines also contain the most liberal statement to date by enforcement officials of the willingness to take account of potential efficiencies that may be realized through mergers. Indeed, the Justice Department relied heavily on efficiency arguments in permitting the revised merger between LTV Corp. and Republic Steel Corp. in 1983. (Frankena and Pautler, *Antitrust Policy for Declining Industries*, p. 93.) Nevertheless, the "efficiencies defense" is still a narrow one. The 1984 guidelines allow it to overcome other evidence of anticompetitive effects only when the parties to the merger can establish with "clear and convincing evidence" that the combination will produce "significant" net efficiencies.

Similarly, the guidelines allow mergers to go forward if they would permit the rescue of a "failing company." However, the criteria for this defense are so restrictive that they afford very little relief to firms in import-damaged industries.

22. See, for example, *International Tel. and Tel. Corp.* v. *General Tire Electronics Corp.*, 351 F. Supp. 1153 (D. Hawaii 1972) (rejecting a world market definition for telephone equipment); *Barry Wright Corp.* v. *Pacific Scientific Corp.*, 555 F. Supp. 1264 (D. Mass. 1983) (limiting the relevant market for shock arresters to the United States). See Frankena and Pautler, *Antitrust Policy for Declining Industries*, pp. 97–98.

current consumption and shipment patterns and then seek to determine what other products or suppliers consumers would turn to if prices changed permanently by a "small but significant" amount. The guidelines use a hypothetical price increase of 5 percent lasting one year on the theory that if competitive responses would cause a price increase this small to be unprofitable, then the geographic area and the group of products should be expanded to take account of this additional competition. If a significant number of consumers switched to sugar substitutes in response to a 5 percent increase in the price of sugar, for example, the guidelines would include both sugar and its substitutes in the same product market. Similarly, if a 5 percent increase in the price of locally produced milk caused milk suppliers from neighboring states to divert sales to the local market, then the guidelines would include the neighboring states with local producers in the same geographic market.

In principle, the approach to market definition contained in the 1984 guidelines makes no distinction between foreign and domestic producers and thus views mergers between firms in highly import-sensitive industries more favorably than under earlier enforcement policy.[23] Specifically, the guidelines indicate that if the data are available, the relevant markets in which American firms are deemed to compete could be measured not only by all existing production and capacity of all domestic competitors, but by all capacity of foreign producers that could be devoted to exports of competing products to the United States in the event prices here increased by the hypothetical 5 percent. This broad approach, of course, would include in the market measure much greater volumes from foreign producers than are evident in current imports. Nevertheless, the 1984 guidelines also recognize that trade restrictions, uncertainties in exchange rates, and other factors can impede the free flow of goods across international boundaries. If such factors exist, even current volumes of foreign goods exported to the United States may overstate their competitive effects on American firms, and the antitrust authorities will recognize these limitations by making appropriate adjustments. The same is true when sufficient data on foreign production capacities are not available, in which case only current shipments of foreign goods to the United States may be considered.

The expansive approach to the definition of geographic markets

23. As the Justice Department's 1984 merger guidelines state in section 2.4, "To the extent available information permits, market shares will be assigned to foreign competitors in the same way in which they are assigned to domestic competitors."

adopted by antitrust enforcers during the Reagan administration represents a good start at recognizing the breadth of competition in markets in which import-sensitive firms compete. The approach is particularly useful for facilitating mergers between firms in industries that have been seriously injured by imports. However, the merger guidelines are only statements of government enforcement policy and are not legally binding.[24]

Whether or not special merger antitrust standards are adopted for import-damaged industries, a strong case exists for amending section 7 of the Clayton Act to reflect the approach to market definition set forth in the new guidelines. The Reagan administration's proposed Merger Modernization Act of 1986 (H.R. 4247 and S. 2160) would do this by modifying section 7 to proscribe mergers only if they create a "significant probability" that one or more firms in the market will be able profitably to "maintain prices above competitive levels for a significant period of time." Substituting the "significant probability" standard for the "may tend to" language now in the Clayton Act would not specifically mandate the use of the analysis of market definition in the 1984 merger guidelines, but it would encourage courts to look favorably on that analysis and thus realistically assess the strength of competition in industries suffering from strong import competition.[25]

Nevertheless, a broad restatement of merger standards may still not ensure special recognition of the strength of foreign competition on domestic industries that the ITC finds have been so hard hit by imports that they have suffered serious economic damage. In such cases, one way in which even the standards reflected in the merger guidelines can be relaxed is to state that in computing the size of the relevant geographic market in which import-damaged firms compete, courts must include all production (and, if the data are available, capacity), *wherever it may be sold,* of foreign firms currently exporting the relevant product to the United States.

Landes and Posner have recently advocated this approach for assess-

24. Although it is still too early to tell how the guidelines will ultimately be received by courts, the reception thus far has been mixed. For the view that the guidelines are authoritative statements on merger law, see *United States* v. *Waste Management Inc.,* 743 F.2d 967, 982–83 (2d Cir. 1984). For a contrary view, see *Montfort of Colorado, Inc.* v. *Cargill, Inc.,* 1985-1 CCH Trade Cas. par. 66,576 (10th Cir. 1985).

25. This effect would be strengthened if the market definition analysis used in the 1984 guidelines were endorsed in the House and Senate reports accompanying any final legislation that adopted the "significant probability" standard.

ing all mergers.[26] They argue that if a distant seller has any sales in a local market, all its sales, wherever made, should be considered as part of the local market for purposes of computing market shares. They reason that once a distant seller, and more specifically a foreign seller, has crossed the transportation cost threshold by making some sales in a market, it can readily expand sales by diverting current shipments to the local market should prices there increase.

The Landes-Posner market-definition test can be criticized for ignoring the difficulties that foreign producers exporting small volumes of goods to the United States may have in diverting significantly greater quantities to American consumers if prices of competing domestic goods increase.[27] However, this criticism is inappropriate for domestic industries that have been ravaged by import competition. If foreign manufacturers can ship such large volumes to the American market that they are able to inflict serious damage on their American competitors, they should be able to reroute to the United States goods destined for other locations or to expand production to meet additional demand if U.S. prices rise. In such circumstances the Landes-Posner assumption that all current production (or capacity, if data are available) by foreign exporters could be sent to the United States would appear to offer a reasonable (albeit liberal) approximation of the true discipline exerted on American firms by their foreign competition, provided the domestic industry is not shielded from import competition by quotas.[28]

The Reagan administration has announced a different approach for relaxing merger standards for import-damaged industries. Under this proposal the president could award firms in industries proving serious injury before the ITC an exemption from the Clayton Act's merger standards for five years, unless there is a "significant probability" that the merger would enable the *resulting* firm to exercise market power.[29] This standard is more liberal than the one the administration recommends

26. William M. Landes and Richard A. Posner, "Market Power in Antitrust Cases," *Harvard Law Review*, vol. 94 (March 1981), pp. 963–65.

27. For general critiques of the Landes-Posner test, see "Comments—Landes and Posner on Market Power: Four Responses," *Harvard Law Review*, vol. 95 (June 1982), pp. 1787–1874.

28. Indeed, even this measure may understate the strength of foreign competition, since it is based solely on foreign firms that may be currently exporting the relevant goods to the United States. Even a small nontransitory price increase could be expected to induce additional foreign producers to begin exporting to the United States.

29. This proposal is embodied in a bill entitled the "Promoting Competition in Distressed Industries Act."

be adopted for all other mergers. That standard would proscribe mergers when there is a significant probability that *one or more* firms in the market will be able to exercise market power. A drawback of the administration's approach is that it would allow a merger of firms in an import-damaged industry that did not create a monopoly but nevertheless could so enhance concentration in a market that it would create a risk of collusion among one or more industry members (which would otherwise violate the general standard). Accordingly, we believe our proposal to apply a more liberal geographic market test when weighing mergers of firms in import-damaged industries is more in keeping with market realities in such circumstances than is changing the section 7 standard itself.

Nevertheless, the risks of either proposal are probably not great. If foreign firms have so successfully penetrated the U.S. market that they have seriously damaged American competitors, the likelihood that any merger between domestic firms here would later create an imperfectly competitive market is remote. As chapter 4 noted, only one of sixteen domestic industries that have received some type of import protection has subsequently returned to the levels of production and employment it enjoyed before protection. This evidence suggests that once imports have seriously damaged an industry, foreign competition will continue to exert a strong disciplining influence. A relaxed merger policy for domestic industries troubled by imports thus runs very low risks, while offering policymakers a way of providing relief that is less harmful to consumers and taxpayers than either quota or tariff protection.

The risks become unacceptable, however, if liberalizing merger standards entails a total exemption from the Clayton Act, even for the five-year escape clause period. A total exemption could let slip through the antitrust net the one or more mergers that would otherwise be challenged by the federal antitrust authorities, even under relaxed merger standards. Experience proves that unscrambling the corporate eggs after a merger is more difficult than keeping them unscrambled by preventing the merger.[30] Any incipient monopolies that would be allowed to form under a broad exemption could harm consumers to a greater degree and for longer periods than either a temporary tariff or quota imposed under the escape clause. A less expansive antitrust option for escape clause

30. It can also take time. For example, the divestiture of AT&T was not agreed upon until seven years after the Justice Department had filed its antitrust suit.

relief could achieve virtually all the benefits of an exemption without running these risks.

### Improving Trade Adjustment Assistance

As we argued in chapter 3, the TAA program has failed either to encourage adjustment or to provide compensation proportional to the economic injury that workers and firms have suffered because of intense import competition. Our suggested revisions in the program are designed to correct both flaws.

First, TAA benefits should be made available automatically to all displaced workers in industries that the ITC finds have suffered serious import-induced injury. If this recommendation were implemented, the Labor Department would not have to certify eligibility for worker assistance except when groups of workers apply to the department directly for TAA benefits (forgoing the potentially costly escape clause process).

Second, the compensation component of our TAA proposal would provide qualified displaced workers with two types of earnings-related payments: earnings insurance for all displaced workers and up to twenty-six weeks of extended unemployment insurance payments for trade-displaced workers residing in regions of high unemployment where alternative jobs may be less plentiful. In addition, any qualified worker choosing to move to obtain new employment would continue to be eligible for a relocation allowance (as under the existing TAA program).

The earnings insurance component of our proposal, which compensates displaced workers only when they accept new employment, is clearly the most important change in the TAA program we recommend. Payments under the program would equal a fixed percentage of any erosion in earnings for a particular period of time. Thus, with a compensation ratio of 50 percent, a displaced worker from a designated industry who had earned $20,000 a year in wages and had accepted a new job with a salary of $10,000 would receive, for a specified period, supplemental payments calculated from a base of $5,000 a year. The proportion of income replaced (the compensation ratio) could decline gradually and reflect the age and experience of individual workers. Junior workers who have built up less human capital in their specific job skills might receive lower replacement rates, for example. Total compensation payments made to any worker over a given period could be subject to a legislated ceiling.[31]

This proposed earnings insurance mechanism, in conjunction with extended unemployment insurance payments for displaced workers in regions of high unemployment, would represent a significant improvement on past and current TAA programs. By providing extra compensation to workers after they find new employment, the proposal would give them an incentive to adjust. Rather than remain idle in the hope of being reemployed by their old firms, workers would more likely accept jobs paying lower wages but offering new career opportunities, training programs, and chances to build seniority.

The proposed compensation plan would be financed out of revenue from tariffs imposed under the escape clause and from those designed to replace existing quotas. The quota conversions, in particular, would be best accomplished in a multilateral framework, perhaps as part of the next round of GATT negotiations. Indeed, the subject of conversion is an ideal one to raise in the context of negotiations to revise and strengthen Article XIX.[32]

The revenues and outlays for our proposed worker compensation plan shown in table 5-1 have been estimated under assumptions purposely designed to be least favorable to financing the program. We have used the most conservative estimates made recently by the staff at the Federal Reserve Bank of New York of the potential revenues from converting only the existing textile, sugar, and steel quotas to tariffs. We then assume these revenues decline over time (fifteen years for textiles and sugar, five years for steel).[33] Outlay estimates, meanwhile, assume that

31. While our earnings compensation program adds to the incentive of a trade-displaced worker to accept new employment, it does reduce the marginal incentive for that worker to switch jobs after becoming eligible for compensation. For example, a trade-displaced autoworker previously earning $30,000 a year who finds a new job paying $10,000 a year and who is eligible for 50 percent compensation would receive $10,000 a year in earnings insurance. This worker would have less incentive under our program to move to another job paying $11,000 because his insurance payment would then decline to $9,500, a reduction representing a 50 percent marginal tax rate, well above the marginal income tax rate this worker must pay. Nevertheless, the incentives to seek new employment under this system would be much superior to incentives under the current TAA program.

32. Our suggestions for reforming Article XIX are discussed above under "Improving the Escape Clause."

33. Susan Hickok, "The Consumer Cost of U.S. Trade Restraints," *Federal Reserve Bank of New York Quarterly Review*, vol. 10 (Summer 1985), pp. 1–12. The conservative

Table 5-1. *Fifteen-Year Projection of Revenue and Outlays for Recommended Trade Adjustment Assistance Program (Worker Compensation Only)*

Billions of current-year dollars

| Item | Year | | | | | | | | | | | | | | |
|---|---|---|---|---|---|---|---|---|---|---|---|---|---|---|---|
| | 1 | 2 | 3 | 4 | 5 | 6 | 7 | 8 | 9 | 10 | 11 | 12 | 13 | 14 | 15 |
| Revenue from quota conversions | | | | | | | | | | | | | | | |
| Textiles | 1.80 | 1.68 | 1.56 | 1.44 | 1.32 | 1.20 | 1.08 | 0.96 | 0.84 | 0.72 | 0.60 | 0.48 | 0.36 | 0.24 | 0.12 |
| Sugar | 0.25 | 0.23 | 0.22 | 0.20 | 0.18 | 0.17 | 0.15 | 0.13 | 0.12 | 0.10 | 0.08 | 0.07 | 0.05 | 0.03 | 0.02 |
| Steel | 0.37 | 0.30 | 0.22 | 0.15 | 0.07 | ... | ... | ... | ... | ... | ... | ... | ... | ... | ... |
| Subtotal | 2.42 | 2.21 | 2.00 | 1.79 | 1.57 | 1.37 | 1.23 | 1.09 | 0.96 | 0.82 | 0.68 | 0.55 | 0.41 | 0.27 | 0.14 |
| Balance from previous year[a] | 0 | 1.72 | 3.30 | 4.73 | 6.00 | 7.08 | 7.98 | 8.74 | 9.35 | 9.81 | 10.09 | 10.17 | 10.04 | 9.68 | 9.05 |
| Total revenues | 2.42 | 3.93 | 5.30 | 6.52 | 7.57 | 8.45 | 9.21 | 9.83 | 10.31 | 10.63 | 10.77 | 10.72 | 10.45 | 9.95 | 9.19 |
| Outlays[b] | 0.83 | 0.87 | 0.92 | 0.96 | 1.01 | 1.06 | 1.11 | 1.17 | 1.23 | 1.29 | 1.35 | 1.42 | 1.49 | 1.57 | 1.64 |
| End-of-year balance | 1.59 | 3.06 | 4.38 | 5.56 | 6.56 | 7.39 | 8.10 | 8.66 | 9.08 | 9.34 | 9.42 | 9.30 | 8.96 | 8.38 | 7.55 |

Sources: Susan Hickok, "The Consumer Cost of U.S. Trade Restraints," *Federal Reserve Bank of New York Quarterly Review*, vol. 10 (Summer 1985), p. 1–12; and authors' estimates.

a. Assumes interest on prior end-of-year balance at 8 percent a year.

b. Escalates at 5 percent a year (for underlying figures, see tables 5-5 and 5-6 in the appendix to this chapter).

430,000 displaced workers would be eligible for some type of assistance each year—294,600 for insurance from wage losses and 135,500 for extended unemployment insurance. For comparison, roughly 250,000 trade-displaced workers, on average, received assistance each year in 1976–80, the peak years of the previous TAA program; the annual average dropped to only 36,000 in 1981–85 (see table 3-6). The outlay projections assume that benefit payments increase at an annual rate of 5 percent a year to reflect both inflation and employment growth and that interest of 8 percent a year is earned on any outstanding balance in the TAA trust fund.

Under these highly conservative assumptions, which are described more fully in the appendix to this chapter, converting existing quotas to tariffs could by itself generate sufficient revenue to fund our recommended worker compensation program without the need for supplemental funds from any new tariffs or from general federal tax revenues. Table 5-1 shows that a trust fund used only to pay for trade adjustment assistance would still have a balance in excess of $7 billion at the end of fifteen years. Table 5-2 shows that a trust fund financed solely by revenues from converting existing quotas to tariffs could also support for more than a decade both generous trade adjustment assistance for workers and a compensation mechanism that provided generous allowances to exporting countries adversely affected by quota-to-tariff conversions.[34] Of course, until the conversion process is completed, it may be necessary to fund the adjustment assistance program out of general revenues.

Any new tariffs that would be imposed under future escape clause proceedings would supplement the revenue from converting existing quotas. Depending on the industry affected, these tariffs could generate sizable sums.

Consider, for example, what would have occurred if a tariff had replaced the VRA that currently limits exports of Japanese autos to the

---

estimates imply gains to the Treasury in the first year of $2.42 billion. If the higher tariff estimates in the New York Federal Reserve study are used, first-year revenues could be as high as $7 billion. Hufbauer and Rosen estimate that the gains from converting quotas to tariffs would exceed $7 billion. (*Trade Policy for Troubled Industries*, chap. 2.)

34. As explained in the appendix to this chapter, the estimates in table 5-2 assume that half of all revenues from quota auctions in the first three years are used for compensating exporting countries and that a third of all tariff revenues in the subsequent twelve years are devoted to compensating the least developed of the exporting countries.

Table 5-2. *Fifteen-Year Projection of Revenue and Outlays for Recommended Trade Adjustment Assistance Program (Country Compensation Included)*
Billions of current-year dollars

| Item | 1 | 2 | 3 | 4 | 5 | 6 | 7 | 8 | 9 | 10 | 11 | 12 | 13 | 14 | 15 |
|---|---|---|---|---|---|---|---|---|---|---|---|---|---|---|---|
| | | | | | | | | Year | | | | | | | |
| Revenue from quota conversions | | | | | | | | | | | | | | | |
| Textiles | 1.80 | 1.80 | 1.80 | 1.80 | 1.65 | 1.50 | 1.35 | 1.20 | 1.05 | 0.90 | 0.75 | 0.60 | 0.45 | 0.30 | 0.15 |
| Sugar | 0.25 | 0.25 | 0.25 | 0.25 | 0.23 | 0.21 | 0.19 | 0.17 | 0.15 | 0.11 | 0.09 | 0.07 | 0.05 | 0.03 | 0.01 |
| Steel | 0.37 | 0.30 | 0.22 | 0.15 | 0.07 | ... | ... | ... | ... | ... | ... | ... | ... | ... | ... |
| Subtotal | 2.42 | 2.35 | 2.27 | 2.20 | 1.95 | 1.71 | 1.54 | 1.37 | 1.20 | 1.01 | 0.84 | 0.67 | 0.50 | 0.33 | 0.16 |
| Balance from previous year[a] | 0 | 0.41 | 0.78 | 1.07 | 1.71 | 2.16 | 2.42 | 2.53 | 2.45 | 2.18 | 1.70 | 0.98 | 0.01 | -1.16 | -2.51 |
| Total revenues | 2.42 | 2.76 | 3.05 | 3.27 | 3.66 | 3.87 | 3.96 | 3.90 | 3.65 | 3.19 | 2.54 | 1.65 | 0.51 | -0.83 | -2.35 |
| Country outlays | 1.21 | 1.17 | 1.14 | 0.73 | 0.65 | 0.57 | 0.51 | 0.46 | 0.40 | 0.33 | 0.28 | 0.22 | 0.18 | 0.11 | 0.05 |
| Worker outlays[b] | 0.83 | 0.87 | 0.92 | 0.96 | 1.01 | 1.06 | 1.11 | 1.17 | 1.23 | 1.29 | 1.35 | 1.42 | 1.49 | 1.57 | 1.64 |
| Total outlays | 2.04 | 2.04 | 2.06 | 1.69 | 1.66 | 1.63 | 1.62 | 1.63 | 1.63 | 1.62 | 1.63 | 1.64 | 1.67 | 1.68 | 1.69 |
| End-of-year balance | 0.38 | 0.72 | 0.99 | 1.58 | 2.00 | 2.24 | 2.34 | 2.27 | 2.02 | 1.57 | 0.91 | 0.01 | -1.16 | -2.51 | -4.04 |

Sources: Same as table 5-1. For assumptions not detailed below, see the appendix to this chapter.
a. Assumes interest on prior end-of-year balance at 8 percent a year.
b. Escalates at 5 percent a year (for underlying figures, see tables 5-5 and 5-6 in the appendix to this chapter).

United States and if the resulting revenues had been used to assist the readjustment of displaced autoworkers. According to the Department of Labor, between January 1979 and January 1984, 225,000 workers were displaced from the U.S. automobile industry. By January 1984, two-thirds of these workers were reemployed at median annual earnings some $4,000 a worker less than before.[35] A tariff providing protection equivalent to that of the VRA would have easily funded a program to compensate for these earnings losses. According to Crandall, the VRA increased the average price of a Japanese car by $1,000 in 1983.[36] The tariff equivalent of this $1,000 increase would have yielded $1.85 billion in revenues. Such a sum not only would have funded full compensation for the annual income erosion of all reemployed autoworkers (a total cost of $603 million) but also would have generated $16,000 for each remaining unemployed worker.

These calculations suggest that even a smaller auto tariff—one that, relative to the VRA, would have provided some relief for American consumers—would have proved more than sufficient to fund our recommended assistance program. According to Crandall, the VRA increased automobile employment in the United States in 1983 by 46,200 jobs.[37] Assuming that a tariff with half the protective effect of the VRA in 1983 would have yielded only half as many jobs, 23,100 workers would have been displaced. However, with a lower tariff, American consumers would have saved at least $500 on each Japanese car purchased and approximately $200 on each American car. And the $925 million in revenue raised by the tariff would have sufficed to offset two-thirds of the income lost by displaced workers reemployed at lower wages (a total cost of $445 million) and would still have yielded $5,860 for each unemployed worker to fund extended unemployment compensation, retraining, and other dislocation assistance. The amounts that would have been available for autoworker compensation would have been even larger if the VRA on autos had been converted to a tariff in 1984, because the estimated price increase on Japanese cars caused by the VRA in that year was as high as $2,500.[38]

35. Paul O. Flaim and Ellen Sehgal, "Displaced Workers of 1979–83: How Well Have They Fared?" *Monthly Labor Review*, vol. 108 (June 1985), pp. 11–13.
36. Robert W. Crandall, "Import Quotas and the Automobile Industry: The Costs of Protectionism," *Brookings Review*, vol. 2 (Summer 1984), pp. 13–16.
37. Ibid., p. 16.
38. Robert W. Crandall, "Detroit Rode Quotas to Prosperity," *Wall Street Journal*, January 29, 1986.

The experience of the automobile industry during the past four years illustrates the advantages of our proposal for quota conversion, particularly because that experience poses a severe test. Given their above-average wages, autoworkers as a group experience relatively large earnings losses. In more typical cases, in which more of the employment displacement would result from imports and workers would suffer less erosion of earnings than autoworkers did, the benefits of the adjustment plan could be even greater and the costs lower.

The final component of our proposed TAA program would aid workers who prefer to enroll in state-certified training programs. Very few trade-displaced workers who have enrolled in retraining programs in the past have subsequently found jobs for which their retraining was intended to qualify them. A major reason was probably that retraining was tied to eligibility for extended unemployment benefits and too few workers took the program seriously. Retraining programs would prove far more effective if they remained truly voluntary and if workers bore at least some portion of their cost—if not immediately, then in future years.[39]

Accordingly, we propose that a combination of grants and loans finance worker retraining under TAA. Repayments of loan obligations would be made directly through workers' tax returns and would begin only after they have surpassed their previous peak wage earnings, as reflected on their earlier tax returns. The proportion of the retraining cost repaid could also vary with their incremental earnings. Those workers exceeding previous earnings by a large percentage could be required to repay a greater proportion of their training costs.

Not only is such a financing mechanism fair, it would also allow workers to obtain financing for retraining efforts without undue burdens. Moreover, requiring trade-displaced workers to have some financial stake in retraining programs would provide strong incentives for these workers to choose retraining carefully, considering both future earnings prospects and employment opportunities. Finally, a contingent loan repayment system—already in effect at some colleges—would allow the government to take "equity" positions in its citizens, that is, share in

39. As a recent Office of Technology Assessment report concluded, "Retraining is not for everyone. Many blue-collar workers who have drawn a paycheck for years simply do not want to go back to the classroom—especially if other jobs are available." OTA, *Technology and Structural Unemployment: Reemploying Displaced Adults, Summary* (Government Printing Office, 1986), p. 7.

the income gains generated by investments in education. Indeed, contingent repayment should be made a feature of other educational and training loan programs.[40]

These proposals should not entail significant administrative complexities. Earnings insurance payments would probably be made most efficiently by the Labor Department, which currently administers both the unemployment insurance and TAA programs. Benefit payment levels could be easily calculated from the W-2 records of trade-displaced workers for their previous and new jobs. The Labor Department could also process and disburse the retraining loans or delegate these functions to the states. The department would notify the Internal Revenue Service of all these loans, since repayment would be made on the basis of a worker's adjusted gross income. There would thus be no need to establish a separate bureaucracy to collect the loans. Instead, the IRS could add a line to the existing form 1040 for workers to include any required repayment in their annual income tax payments.

## Assisting Communities

A major source of political pressure for protection stems from concern about the impact of major plant closures on particular communities. Given the large fixed overhead costs of schools, utilities, and police and fire services, communities that experience plant closures must often add the insult of additional taxes to the injury of an already shrinking populace. Although the concern for these effects has influenced the design of the trade adjustment assistance program, aid to impacted communities has been virtually nonexistent. The only mechanism for helping these communities has been legislation adopted in a number of states requiring companies to provide advance notice of plant closings.

A new, positive approach is needed to assist communities adversely affected by structural changes in the economy. The approach should not rely on general appropriations, which have proved a poor way to target regional assistance. Programs for aiding distressed regions, such as the model cities initiative and the work of the Economic Development

40. Congressman Thomas E. Petri (R-Wis.) has introduced legislation (H.R. 2733) to create a National Student Loan Bank, which would issue contingent income repayment loans directly from the Treasury.

Administration, have tended to expand beyond their original purposes.

Under our approach, communities would voluntarily choose to insure their tax bases against sudden erosion rather than to depend on a government grant program. The insurance program might, for example, allow a city experiencing an annual loss of more than 5 percent of its tax revenues for reasons other than rate reductions to recover from a government-administered insurance pool some proportion of that loss. The percentage threshold for losses to the tax base would vary by community size; a lower percentage loss would be required for larger cities, where even the closing of a large plant may have a relatively small effect on the tax base. Insurance premiums paid by communities electing to join the program would finance the pool. Because the insurance coverage would extend to all sudden diminutions in a community's tax base, all types of communities, not just those experiencing steady long-term population erosions, would be encouraged to participate.[41]

We have considered the costs of running such a program on a self-financing basis for thirty-eight sample counties with populations exceeding 100,000. The costs were based on Commerce Department data for fiscal 1973 to 1983. Because Michigan has experienced considerable difficulties during the period, we felt it would present an interesting case.[42] We added ten counties (in alphabetical order) drawn from Texas and Pennsylvania to provide geographic diversity. The cost of our program would depend on the percentage decline in the tax base that triggered the payments, the proportion of the decline that was reimbursed, and the duration of the payments. We modeled programs that would compensate counties for half the erosion in their tax bases with payments triggered by annual shortfalls in excess of 5 and 10 percent in both nominal and real terms.

As tables 5-3 and 5-4 show, the tax-base insurance plan could have been implemented at relatively low cost. In the most expensive case, insurance that compensated counties for short-term declines in the tax

41. However, those communities that have suffered tax-base losses in excess of the insurance threshold in several years during, say, the past decade could be required to wait for a year or two before becoming eligible. This eligibility period could reduce the tendency of a tax-base insurance program to attract primarily high-risk communities.

42. For an excellent discussion of the Michigan experience, see Task Force for a Long-Term Economic Strategy for Michigan, *The Path to Prosperity: Findings and Recommendations of the Task Force for a Long-Term Economic Strategy for Michigan* (Ann Arbor: The Task Force, 1984).

Table 5-3. *Distribution of Eligibility of Thirty-eight Counties under Four Scenarios of Proposed Tax-Base Insurance Program, 1973–82*[a]

| | Number of times counties are eligible for insurance in ten-year period | | | | | | |
|---|---|---|---|---|---|---|---|
| Scenario | 0 | 1 | 2 | 3 | 4 | 5 | 6 |
| Nominal loss greater than 5 percent | 21 | 15 | 1 | 1 | 0 | 0 | 0 |
| Nominal loss greater than 10 percent | 33 | 4 | 0 | 1 | 0 | 0 | 0 |
| Real loss greater than 5 percent | 2 | 6 | 8 | 9 | 9 | 3 | 1 |
| Real loss greater than 10 percent | 13 | 8 | 14 | 3 | 0 | 0 | 0 |

Sources: Calculations based on data from U.S. Bureau of the Census, *County Government Finance in 1982–83*, table 5, and earlier issues.

a. Entries are number of counties eligible under each scenario. The sample of thirty-eight counties consists of eighteen counties in Michigan and ten randomly selected counties in both Pennsylvania and Texas. All thirty-eight counties had populations of more than 100,000 from 1972 to 1982, except Livingston County, Michigan.

base in excess of 5 percent in real terms would have had broad use—all but two counties would have received revenues on at least one occasion. But in most cases the shortfall in the tax base would have been between 5 and 15 percent. The total payments under a program that compensated for more than a 5 percent decline in the real tax base would have amounted to about 0.5 percent of the overall tax revenues received by these counties. Because an insurance fund can earn income on premiums before making disbursements, a self-financing program could charge premiums that were lower than this cost estimate.[43] Protecting communities for half the losses greater than 10 percent in real terms would have cost 0.15 percent of total revenues, while protection from half the losses greater than 5 and 10 percent declines in nominal tax revenues would have cost 0.05 and 0.01 percent of revenues respectively.

It is possible, of course, to confine such a program to trade-related losses to the tax base, which would presumably have reduced costs even further. A mechanism similar to the section 201 procedure for trade-

43. The use of actual revenue data for these simulations is not ideal. In the first place, the data could reflect the impact of tax-rate reductions that the program would not cover. This would bias the cost estimates upward. On the other hand, in the face of shortfalls, counties that raised tax rates might not have done so if a tax-base insurance program had been in effect.

Table 5-4. *Estimated Cost of Proposed Tax-Base Insurance Program as a Percentage of Total Tax Revenues, 1973–82*[a]

| Amount of shortfall in tax revenues | Nominal | Real |
|---|---|---|
| More than 5 percent decline | 0.049 | 0.507 |
| More than 10 percent decline | 0.010 | 0.146 |

Sources: Calculations based on data from Bureau of the Census, *County Government Finance in 1982–83*, table 5, and earlier issues.

a. Tax revenues are those of the thirty-eight counties described in the note to table 5-3. Costs are based on compensating each county for one-half its tax revenue loss of 5 or 10 percent. Estimates reflect the sum of year-to-year changes over a ten-year period.

injured industries could be established to determine the causal role of trade in regional economic injury. However, given the voluntary and potentially self-financing nature of the tax-base insurance plan, no reason exists in principle or practice why the program should be so restricted.

Finally, the governmental entities or levels insured would have to be clearly determined if the tax-base insurance mechanism were established. We are not wedded to any particular concept. Municipalities, counties, or state governments could be eligible. We suspect, however, that the final choice would depend on the availability of reliable tax-base data.

## Conclusion

For free traders, these are dangerous times. Pressures to adopt protectionist measures either in specific sectors or in generic trade legislation are as intense as they have been at any time in the postwar era. But both the nation and the intended beneficiaries of protectionist devices themselves would commit a serious mistake by yielding to these pressures. Proposals to use the trade laws as a vehicle for implementing an industrial policy for declining industries are equally misguided.

The most attractive course is to strengthen existing institutions to absorb demands for protectionist actions, but to do so only in a cost-effective manner. The proposals advanced in this concluding chapter fulfill this objective and, together with appropriate corrections in fiscal policy, can help place the U.S. economy on a path of sustainable growth without permanent protection.

## Appendix: Assumptions for Revenue and Outlay Projections for the Worker Assistance Program

This appendix describes the principal assumptions used in constructing the revenue and outlay estimates for our recommended trade adjustment assistance program that are shown in tables 5-1 and 5-2.

### Revenue Projections

The initial revenue estimates from converting existing textile, sugar, and steel quotas are drawn from the New York Federal Reserve Bank.[44] When exporting countries are not to be compensated for losses in quota rents, our projections assume that the tariffs on textiles and sugar phase out over fifteen years and the steel tariffs (which would replace the recently negotiated VRAs on steel products) phase out over five years. These assumptions are modified when exporting countries are given some compensation, so that revenues from auctioning quotas and tariffs are assumed to be constant for the first four years and revenues from tariffs thereafter to phase out over the next eleven years. Our revenue estimates are conservative; they do not make allowances for increases in the level of imports, which would be expected as domestic incomes increase and prices fall because of the declining level of overall protection.

### Outlay Projections for Worker Assistance

Outlay projections are based on the job displacement survey covering 1979–83 that was performed by the Bureau of Labor Statistics.[45] Specifically, we make the liberal assumption that the number of workers who would be eligible for wage loss payments in future years would equal half of all manufacturing workers who were displaced between 1979 and 1983 (which, however, assumes no growth in unemployment levels). We further assume that each displaced worker receives compensation for two years equal to 50 percent of the median loss in wages in his or her new job. On an annual basis, these assumptions translate into 294,600

44. Hickok, "Consumer Cost of U.S. Trade Restraints," pp. 1–12.
45. Flaim and Sehgal, "Displaced Workers of 1979–83," pp. 3–16.

Table 5-5. *Estimated Outlays for Wage Insurance of Workers Displaced during 1979–83*

| | Manufacturing sector | |
|---|---|---|
| Item | Durables | Nondurables |
| Total workers who subsequently found new jobs[a] | 980,000 | 493,000 |
| Annual average | 196,000 | 98,600 |
| Number eligible for wage loss payments[b] | 98,000 | 49,300 |
| Number compensated (2-year duration) | 196,000 | 98,600 |
| Amount of compensation per worker (in dollars)[c] | 1,846 | 260 |
| Total outlays (thousands of dollars) | 361,800 | 25,600 |
| Grand total (thousands of dollars) | 387,400 | |

Sources: Number of displaced workers and median wage loss data from Paul O. Flaim and Ellen Sehgal, "Displaced Workers of 1979–83: How Well Have They Fared?" *Monthly Labor Review*, vol. 108 (June 1985), p. 11; and authors' estimates.
a. As of January 1, 1984.
b. Assumes 50 percent of workers are trade-displaced.
c. Assumes compensation of 50 percent of median wage loss.

workers a year. The estimated steady-state outlays under these assumptions (after the first year) are shown in table 5-5.

We also make the highly liberal assumption that the number of workers who would be eligible for extended unemployment insurance benefits would be equal to 40 percent of all displaced manufacturing workers who were unemployed for less than one year as of January 1984. The 40 percent figure reflects the total number of displaced workers who were unemployed on that date and resided in the three regions of the country with the highest rates of unemployment. Under these assumptions, 135,500 workers would qualify each year for extended unemployment payments, which we assume would equal, on average, 40 percent of previous wages and be paid for six months beyond regular unemployment payments. The estimated first-year outlays for extended unemployment benefits are shown in table 5-6.

Our outlay estimates assume that a total of 430,100 workers would receive some type of benefits each year.

*Outlay Projections for Country Compensation*

Table 5-2 in the text reports outlay estimates for our proposed compensation system for exporting countries that are harmed by any quota-to-tariff conversion. During the first three years, we assume that 50 percent of the total revenues from the auctioned quotas are dedicated

Table 5-6. *Estimated Outlays for Extended Unemployment Insurance of Workers Displaced during 1979–83*

| Item | Manufacturing sector | |
| --- | --- | --- |
| | *Durables* | *Nondurables* |
| Total workers unemployed as of January 1, 1984 | 706,000 | 335,000 |
| Workers unemployed less than one year[a] | 459,000 | 218,000 |
| Number unemployed in high-unemployment areas[b] | 184,000 | 87,000 |
| Number eligible for unemployment insurance benefits each year[c] | 92,000 | 43,500 |
| Amount of compensation per worker (in dollars)[d] | 3,578 | 2,746 |
| Total outlays (thousands of dollars) | 329,200 | 119,500 |
| Grand total (thousands of dollars) | 448,700 | |

Sources: Data on total unemployed and on median earnings from Flaim and Sehgal, "Displaced Workers, 1979–83," pp. 8, 12; and authors' estimates.

a. Number unemployed longer than one year is assumed to be equal to proportion of all unemployed displaced workers who dropped out of the labor force, or about 35 percent.

b. Assumed to be 40 percent of nation.

c. Assumes 50 percent of workers are trade-displaced.

d. Assumes 40 percent compensation of median earnings for six months.

to compensating all exporting nations affected by the conversions. Thereafter, we assume that the quotas are converted to tariffs (in the fourth year) and phased out during the next eleven years, with one-third of the total revenues used for compensating the least developed exporting nations.

# Index

Adams, Walter, 47n
Aho, C. Michael, 13–14n, 15n, 24
Aid programs: criteria for cost-effective, 27–33, 40; direct, 15, 53, 61; equity-based, 12–16; justification for, 13, 26–33; supplemental, 13, 28, 52–53, 55–57. *See also* Trade adjustment assistance (TAA) programs
Airline industry, 25, 37, 68
Anderson, Douglas P., 95n
Antitrust laws: cartelization and, 92, 102; exemptions from, 93–94; sovereign compulsion doctrine and, 4, 102
Article XIX, GATT, 9, 25, 35–37, 39; causation standards, 79–81; circumvention of, 50; compensation requirement, 4, 83, 97; nondiscrimination and, 97; provisions of, 7, 83; quota conversions and, 113; reform of, 4–5, 51n, 102–03; VRAs and, 50
Auction, of import or quota rights. *See* Quotas
Australia: TAA program, 51n; VRAs with, 42n, 90n
Automation, 66, 75, 77
Automobile industry: displaced workers, 28n, 55, 117; *1980* injury case, 50, 81; plant closings in, 72; quotas and, 24, 115, 117–18; VRAs in, 28, 31, 50, 73–74, 76, 81; wages in, 15
Automotive Products Trade Act of *1965*, 54n
Avery, David, 72n

Balance of trade. *See* Deficit, trade
Baldwin, Robert E., 45, 47n, 73n, 74n, 98
Ball-bearing industry, 87
Bankruptcy model, 84–85
*Barry Wright Corp.* v. *Pacific Scientific Corp.*, 107n
Baughman, Laura Megna, 69n
Bayard, Thomas O., 15n, 24

Berliner, Diane T., 47–48
Bhagwati, Jagdish N., 14n, 42n, 57n
Bicycle industry, 10; expansion in, 47; plant relocation in, 87; protection of, 71
Bosworth, Barry P., 18n, 32n
Brazil, VRA with, 90n
Browne, Lynn E., 12n
Burke-Hartke bill, 42

Canada, 42n, 54n
Capital: for labor, 72; markets, 19; misallocation of, 89–91; taxes on income, 21
Carbon products, 46, 87, 90. *See also* Steel industry
Carnevale, Anthony Patrick, 61n
Carpeting industry, 86–87
Carron, Andrew S., 32n
Cartels, 65; crisis, 73; dangers of, 91–96; export, 4; Japanese, 95–96. *See also* Mergers
Carter, Jimmy, 55
Cassing, James, 20n
Caves, Richard E., 17n
Cedar shakes and shingles. *See* Roofing materials industry
Charnovitz, Steve, 52n
Chiles, Lawton, 63–64, 100n
Chrysler Corporation, 85
Clayton Act, 106, 109, 111–12
Cline, William R., 51n
Clothing industry, 15; adjustment strategies, 88; automation and, 66; quotas in, 49; work force of, 94. *See also* Textile industry
Commerce, Department of: 17n, 44, 85–86; community assistance and, 55; TAA and, 53
Communities, TAA programs for, 55, 119–22
Comparative advantage principle, 16, 87–88
Compensation: for exporting countries, 125; GATT, 4, 83, 97

127